Gays in the military

DATE DUE

Gays in the Military

Other Books in the Current Controversies Series

America's Teachers
Assisted Suicide
Developing Nations
Drug Trafficking
Espionage and Intelligence
The Global Impact of Social Media
Government Corruption
The Iranian Reform Movement
Illegal Immigration
The Middle East
Nuclear Armament
Politics and The Media
Pollution
The Tea Party Movement
The Uninsured
Vaccines

| Gays in the Military

Debra A. Miller, Book Editor

GREENHAVEN PRESS
A part of Gale, Cengage Learning

NEW ENGLAND INSTITUTE OF TECHNOLOGY
LIBRARY

GALE
CENGAGE Learning·

Detroit • New York • San Francisco • New Haven, Conn • Waterville, Maine • London

Elizabeth Des Chenes, *Managing Editor*

© 2012 Greenhaven Press, a part of Gale, Cengage Learning

Gale and Greenhaven Press are registered trademarks used herein under license.

For more information, contact:
Greenhaven Press
27500 Drake Rd.
Farmington Hills, MI 48331-3535
Or you can visit our Internet site at gale.cengage.com

Articles in Greenhaven Press anthologies are often edited for length to meet page requirements. In addition, original titles of these works are changed to clearly present the main thesis and to explicitly indicate the author's opinion. Every effort is made to ensure that Greenhaven Press accurately reflects the original intent of the authors. Every effort has been made to trace the owners of copyrighted material.

Cover image copyright © Brian Cahn/ZUMA Press/Corbis.

LIBRARY OF CONGRESS CATALOGING-IN-PUBLICATION DATA

Gays in the military / Debra A. Miller, book editor.
    p. cm. -- (Current controversies)
Includes bibliographical references and index.
ISBN 978-0-7377-5618-0 (hardcover) -- ISBN 978-0-7377-5619-7 (pbk.)
1. Gay military personnel--United States. I. Miller, Debra A.
UB418.G38G3726 2012
355.3'3086640973--dc23

                                                                  2011029030

Printed in the United States of America
1 2 3 4 5 6 7 15 14 13 12 11

Contents

Chapter 1: Should Gays Be Permitted to Serve Openly in the US Military?

Yes: Gays Should Be Permitted to Serve Openly in the US Military

While in the middle of two wars, President Barack Obama wants to require the military to carry out gay rights—a major sociological change that is contrary to the preferences of many military members. Now is not the time to abandon the "Don't Ask Don't Tell" policy.

Chapter 2: Will Repeal of "Don't Ask Don't Tell" Harm the US Military?

No: Repeal of "Don't Ask Don't Tell" Will Not Harm the US Military

Chapter 3: Do Members of the Military Support Ending "Don't Ask Don't Tell"?

Homosexuals have long served in the military covertly, but repeal of "Don't Ask Don't Tell" could cause major problems if openly gay service members are housed in barracks with heterosexuals.

Foreword

By definition, controversies are "discussions of questions in which opposing opinions clash" (Webster's Twentieth Century Dictionary Unabridged). Few would deny that controversies are a pervasive part of the human condition and exist on virtually every level of human enterprise. Controversies transpire between individuals and among groups, within nations and between nations. Controversies supply the grist necessary for progress by providing challenges and challengers to the status quo. They also create atmospheres where strife and warfare can flourish. A world without controversies would be a peaceful world; but it also would be, by and large, static and prosaic.

The Series' Purpose

The purpose of the Current Controversies series is to explore many of the social, political, and economic controversies dominating the national and international scenes today. Titles selected for inclusion in the series are highly focused and specific. For example, from the larger category of criminal justice, Current Controversies deals with specific topics such as police brutality, gun control, white collar crime, and others. The debates in Current Controversies also are presented in a useful, timeless fashion. Articles and book excerpts included in each title are selected if they contribute valuable, long-range ideas to the overall debate. And wherever possible, current information is enhanced with historical documents and other relevant materials. Thus, while individual titles are current in focus, every effort is made to ensure that they will not become quickly outdated. Books in the Current Controversies series will remain important resources for librarians, teachers, and students for many years.

In addition to keeping the titles focused and specific, great care is taken in the editorial format of each book in the series. Book introductions and chapter prefaces are offered to provide background material for readers. Chapters are organized around several key questions that are answered with diverse opinions representing all points on the political spectrum. Materials in each chapter include opinions in which authors clearly disagree as well as alternative opinions in which authors may agree on a broader issue but disagree on the possible solutions. In this way, the content of each volume in Current Controversies mirrors the mosaic of opinions encountered in society. Readers will quickly realize that there are many viable answers to these complex issues. By questioning each author's conclusions, students and casual readers can begin to develop the critical thinking skills so important to evaluating opinionated material.

Current Controversies is also ideal for controlled research. Each anthology in the series is composed of primary sources taken from a wide gamut of informational categories including periodicals, newspapers, books, U.S. and foreign government documents, and the publications of private and public organizations. Readers will find factual support for reports, debates, and research papers covering all areas of important issues. In addition, an annotated table of contents, an index, a book and periodical bibliography, and a list of organizations to contact are included in each book to expedite further research.

Perhaps more than ever before in history, people are confronted with diverse and contradictory information. During the Persian Gulf War, for example, the public was not only treated to minute-to-minute coverage of the war, it was also inundated with critiques of the coverage and countless analyses of the factors motivating U.S. involvement. Being able to sort through the plethora of opinions accompanying today's major issues, and to draw one's own conclusions, can be a complicated and frustrating struggle. It is the editors' hope that Current Controversies will help readers with this struggle.

Introduction

"[Historically,] gays have only been able to serve [in the US military] by hiding their homosexual status, due to anti-gay attitudes within the military, outright bans on gay service, or most recently, the 'Don't Ask Don't Tell' policy, which allowed gays to serve as long as they did not reveal their homosexuality."

The history of gays, or homosexuals, serving in the US military is a contradictory one. On the one hand, there is evidence that gays have served as soldiers and in other military roles throughout the country's history, including during the American Revolution, World War II, and more recent modern wars. On the other hand, during most of that history, gays have only been able to serve by hiding their homosexuality because of antigay attitudes within the military, explicit bans on homosexuals in the armed services, or under the 1993 "Don't Ask Don't Tell" policy, which allowed gays to serve as long as they did not reveal their homosexuality, and which did not allow the military to ask whether they were gay. In late 2010, however, the US Congress repealed "Don't Ask Don't Tell," finally permitting gays to serve openly in the US armed forces—a decision hailed as a great victory by gay rights activists.

For much of early US military history, there was no explicit, written policy concerning gays serving in the military; however, sodomy—the term used for sexual relations between persons of the same sex—was long considered a crime under civilian law, and gay soldiers were dismissed from the military under such laws. Various commentators have reported that the first dismissal of a homosexual American soldier was in 1776, when General George Washington dishonorably discharged Lieutenant Frederick Gotthold Enslin for sodomy and perjury—meaning he was gay and lied about it. The US military explicitly prohibited homosexuality in the Articles of War of 1916, which included "assault with the intent to commit sodomy" as a capital crime. Beginning in World War II, this provision was used as the basis for discharging homosexual soldiers, whether or not they engaged in homosexual acts.

Also, during World War II, the Korean War, and the Vietnam War, the military defined homosexuality as a mental defect, and many homosexual men and women were barred from entering the military if they revealed their homosexual status during recruitment interviews or medical exams. The military developed procedures for spotting gays—such as effeminate body characteristics, dress, or mannerisms—and used these criteria for excluding thousands of recruits who sought to enlist during World War II. During the Vietnam conflict, a highly unpopular war, however, the tables turned, and many draftees tried to appear to be homosexual in order to escape military service.

In 1982, during the administration of President Ronald Reagan, the US Department of Defense issued an outright ban on gays serving in the military—Defense Directive 1332.14, which stated that "homosexuality is incompatible with military service." According to a 1992 report by the Government Accounting (now Accountability) Office, close to seventeen thousand gay men and women were discharged under this policy during the 1980s.

The ban on gays in the military continued until the 1990s, when President Bill Clinton sought to allow qualified persons to serve regardless of their sexual orientation. Gay and lesbian advocates had made this issue a political priority, and attitudes among the American public had begun to change on the subject. President Clinton's efforts, however, met with strong resistance from the Republican-controlled Congress, which threatened to pass a legislative ban on gay service. The standoff resulted in a compromise law that was labeled "Don't Ask Don't Tell," part of the National Defense Authorization Act for 1994, which was signed into law on November 30, 1993. Under this law, military applicants could not be asked about their sexual orientation during recruitment. This meant that gays who kept their homosexuality a secret could serve in the military, but they could not engage in homosexual activities or tell anyone about their sexual orientation.

Although the military, under "Don't Ask Don't Tell," purportedly made certain exceptions—respecting private communications between gay service members and their families and friends, and allowing for the confidential disclosure of homosexuality to defense attorneys, chaplains, security clearance personnel, and doctors who are treating patients for HIV—gay service members have reported that doctors and others often revealed these confidential communications to commanding officers. Gay soldiers also have reported being the victims of harassment and assault by fellow service members who threatened to reveal their homosexual status. And since the military continued to investigate charges that certain service members were gay, these threats were real. In fact, many thousands of military members were dismissed because of their sexual orientation in the years after "Don't Ask Don't Tell" was adopted.

The next president to take up the cause of gays in the military was Barack Obama. Obama first declared his desire to end "Don't Ask Don't Tell" during his presidential campaign in 2008, and in his first State of the Union address in 2010 he reiterated his commitment to finally repeal the law, stating, "This year, I will work with Congress and our military to finally repeal the law that denies gay Americans the right to serve the country they love because of who they are. It's the right thing to do."[1] Shortly thereafter, Secretary of Defense Robert Gates and the chairman of the Joint Chiefs of Staff,

Mike Mullen, voiced their support for repeal in testimony before the Senate Armed Services Committee. On March 2, 2010, Secretary Gates announced that he was ordering the Pentagon to conduct a comprehensive review of the repeal of Don't Ask Don't Tell to examine issues associated with repeal and to include an implementation plan to address any anticipated impacts on the military. As part of the review, the Pentagon sent out a survey to four hundred thousand active-duty and reserve service members, soliciting their views on the impact of repealing Don't Ask Don't Tell.

Throughout 2010, Congress debated the idea of repealing Don't Ask Don't Tell. The House of Representatives passed a repeal bill in May 2010, but repeal legislation stalled in the Senate largely because of opposition from senator and former Republican presidential candidate John McCain. In late November 2010, the Pentagon published its comprehensive report, finding that repeal posed a low risk of harm to the military. Despite the Pentagon findings, however, heads of the army, air force, and marines testified against repeal, claiming that it would cause difficulties for combat troops at a time when the country was still involved in two wars. Yet the significant opposition to repeal was finally overcome when both the House and the Senate passed the Don't Ask Don't Tell Repeal Act of 2010, and the president signed it into law on December 22, 2010. Implementation, however, was delayed until the president, the secretary of defense, and the chairman of the Joint Chiefs of Staff certified that the appropriate regulations had been drafted and that implementation would not harm military readiness or effectiveness, unit cohesion, or recruiting and retention. In January 2011, Secretary Gates released the Defense Department's implementation plan, emphasizing the need for training at all levels of the military.

The issue of homosexuals in the US military is the subject of *Current Controversies: Gays in the Military*. Authors of viewpoints in this volume present a range of views about whether gays should be permitted to serve openly in the military, whether repeal of Don't Ask Don't Tell will harm the US military, whether members of the military support repeal, and what the impact will be of gays serving openly in the military.

Notes

1. Mike Brewer, "Don't Ask Don't Tell Timeline," *Tucson Citizen.com*, December 3, 2010. http://tucsoncitizen.com.

CHAPTER 1

Should Gays Be Permitted to Serve Openly in the US Military?

Chapter Preface

Although US public opinion about homosexuality has become more accepting in recent years, some Americans continue to hold strong antigay attitudes. A compelling example of gay-bashing is revealed in the facts surrounding a 2011 US Supreme Court decision in *Snyder v. Phelps*. The case involved the funeral of US Marine Lance Corporal Matthew Snyder, who died fighting in Iraq on March 3, 2006. Snyder's father, Albert Snyder, held the funeral in Westminster, Maryland, on March 10, 2006. Although Matthew was not a homosexual, his funeral was picketed by members of a tiny, antigay Christian group founded by the Reverend Fred Phelps at the Westboro Baptist Church in Topeka, Kansas. The Phelps group practices a fundamentalist type of religion that holds that God hates gays and lesbians and punishes America for its tolerance of gays, particularly in the US military. The group pickets the funerals of US soldiers to bring attention to its antigay cause.

Neither Matthew Snyder nor his father had ever met the Phelps people, but Rev. Phelps, his daughters, and grandaughters traveled from Kansas to Snyder's Maryland funeral to express their disapproval of gays in the US military. Although the Phelps family members complied with local ordinances and police instructions and stood approximately a thousand feet away from the funeral, they held signs containing messages such as "God Hates the USA," "You're Going to Hell," and "Thank God for Dead Soldiers." The group had made similar appearances at hundreds of other funerals over the past several years.

Albert Snyder reportedly never saw the protesters during the funeral but he later learned about the demonstration from TV coverage. His response was a federal lawsuit claiming invasion of privacy, intrusion upon seclusion, and intentional infliction of emotional distress. At trial, Mr. Snyder testified that the protests caused him emotional harm and exacerbated the grief and depression he felt over the loss of his son. The US District Court for the District of Maryland, following a jury trial, awarded Mr. Snyder $2.9 million in compensatory damages as well as $8 million in punitive damages. The punitive damages were later reduced to $2.1 million by the district court judge. Rev. Phelps appealed to the US Court of Appeals for the Fourth Circuit in Richmond, Virginia, and the appellate court reversed the district court ruling and award of damages, holding that the protests by Phelps and his family were protected speech under the First Amendment to the US Constitution. The appeals court explained that the messages on the protest signs did not refer to Matthew Snyder personally, but were about issues of public concern, namely whether gays should serve in the US military. The court said the Phelpses simply used strong rhetoric designed to spark public debate.

Snyder appealed the case to the US Supreme Court and, after hearing arguments, the Court ruled on March 2, 2011, that the First Amendment protected the antigay protests staged by the Phelpses. The majority opinion, written by chief justice John Roberts, noted that the protesters' signs referred to public rather than private matters—matters that are protected by the First Amendment. The court acknowledged that the protests added to Albert Snyder's grief but found it significant that the protesters stayed a thousand feet away so that they could barely be seen by funeral attendees. Even hurtful speech involving public issues, the court concluded, must be protected in our democracy to ensure that public debate is not stifled. The Supreme Court decision was almost unanimous; the lone dissenter was Samuel Alito, who argued in a dissenting opinion that there are numerous limits on the freedom of speech, and that Matthew Snyder's funeral was a private one that should have been accorded protection from public protests.

The Supreme Court's decision was upsetting to the families of soldiers and veterans. Albert Snyder's assessment of the high court's ruling was that the "eight justices don't have the common sense God gave a goat. . . . We found out today we can no longer bury our dead in this country with dignity."[1] Other reactions varied, with some people supporting the First Amendment ruling and others criticizing it. Many commentators felt the Supreme Court had it right and that the outcome was not surprising—that free speech must be protected because it is one of the democratic freedoms that soldiers like Matthew Snyder fight for. Many others, however, berated the court for its failure to protect families holding private funerals for soldiers who gave their lives to defend their country. Some gay advocates noted the irony in the decision—that US law protects hate groups like the Phelps family but as of March 2011 did not fully protect gays and lesbians serving in the US military.

The authors of the viewpoints in this chapter debate the central issue protested by the Phelps family in 2006—whether gays should be permitted to serve openly in the US military.

Notes

1. The Associated Press, "Supreme Court: Anti-Gay Funeral Picketers Allowed," March 3, 2011. www.npr.org.

Gays in the Military Should Not Have to Live in Fear

Michelle Benecke

*Michelle Benecke served as an army captain and battery com-
mander. She is a founder and former executive director of Servicemembers Legal Defense Network, which seeks repeal of the
military's "Don't Ask Don't Tell" policy.*

In the debate surrounding "don't ask, don't tell" [DADT], we
have heard from most everyone except those harmed by
this law.

DADT silences gay military members and cloaks the fear-
ful reality of what it means to live under this law. As senators
decide how to cast their votes, they should consider the experience of gay military members—and repeal this law.

Living in Fear

Gay military members are not afraid to fight for our country.
Many have given their lives in her service. Every day, however,
they live in fear of "don't ask, don't tell"—of being outed
against their will, dishonored in their community and kicked
out of their profession.

Under DADT, military members are not permitted to con-
fide in parents, friends, doctors—anyone. Many have been discharged after a parent or sibling broke their confidence, often
unwittingly, and the information fell into malevolent hands.
Confiding in a diary is risky, as these have been seized—along
with private letters and emails from private accounts—and
used against numerous military members.

Contrary to what opponents suggest, it is not enough to
"just shut up." Every day, gay men and women are asked in

the course of normal conversations, "Do you have a girlfriend back home?" "Where did you go on leave?"

These seemingly innocuous questions are fraught with risk. Gay military members expend an enormous amount of energy trying to dodge conversations, keeping people at arm's length. But, at the same time, soldiers who do not participate in the usual banter get noticed.

Ultimately, gay military members must create a heterosexual persona, pretending to be someone they are not. Creating a heterosexual dating history is a must. They must keep their silence when confronted by derogatory comments about gay people.

Ultimately, gay military members must create a heterosexual persona, pretending to be someone they are not.

On a more insidious note, many women endure unwanted advances and do not report sexual harassment, given the high likelihood they will be accused of being lesbians in retaliation.

Let Gays Serve with Integety

Most gay military members are little interested in coming out publicly. Rather, repealing DADT would allow military members to serve with integrity, consistent with the military's core values. They could defend themselves if harassed. And, they could enjoy relationships with family members and close friends—not fear them.

We are at a pivotal moment. If DADT is not repealed now, it could be years before this makes its way back to the national fore. Gay military members must live in constant fear as they guard against "friendly fire" under DADT, even as they risk their lives fighting in Iraq and Afghanistan.

The time for repeal is now. Let gay military members serve with honor, integrity—and their voices.

The Ban on Gays Serving Openly in the Military Is Costly for Taxpayers

United Press International

United Press International is a global news service and a leading provider of critical information to media outlets, businesses, governments, and researchers worldwide.

A more open approach to homosexual or bisexual men and women serving in the military will save hundreds of millions of tax dollars and draw more people into the ranks, the Williams Institute at the University of California at Los Angeles [UCLA] said in a research brief made public [January 27, 2010].

The UCLA research body said that U.S. Census figures showed that about 66,000 lesbian, gay and bisexual [LGB] men and women were on military payrolls. The current policy requires members of the armed forces to remain silent about their sexual orientation.

However, the Don't Ask/Don't Tell policy carries huge costs for the taxpayer, the study said. The institute estimated that lifting the DADT policy would attract 50,000 new entrants to the armed forces and save taxpayers huge amounts currently spent on maintaining that policy.

An end to the policy was one of the election pledges made by President Barack Obama. Although Obama has said he wants to push ahead with an end to the ban on openly homosexual relationships in the military, a timetable for a change in the law is still awaited.

"I will end 'Don't Ask Don't Tell,'" Obama said at the annual dinner of the Human Rights Campaign, a gay civil rights advocacy group, but did not specify how and when.

The law was passed by Congress in 1993 and signed by President Bill Clinton, who also promised to repeal the ban on homosexuals in the military. Clinton was thwarted by opposition in both the military and Congress.

Analysts said an underlying difficulty was a deep-rooted culture of machismo in both the military and security industries that transcended international borders.

The Don't Ask/Don't Tell policy carries huge costs for the taxpayer.

Gary J. Gates, Williams distinguished scholar and study author, said, "Despite official policy requiring that lesbians, gay men, and bisexuals remain silent about their sexual orientation, data from the U.S. Census Bureau suggest that an estimated 66,000 LGB men and women are serving in the U.S. military."

The study updated previously published estimates of the cost of the DADT policy made by the Government Accountability Office and the Palm Center at the University of California, Santa Barbara.

According to Gates, ending the ban on openly homosexual relationships in the military will save "a substantial amount of taxpayer dollars since estimates suggest that the policy has cost more than half a billion dollars."

The estimated 66,000 lesbians, gay men and bisexuals cited as current members of the armed forces account for about 2.2 percent of military personnel.

Of those, about 13,000 are serving on active duty and thus comprise 0.9 percent of all active-duty personnel. The remaining 53,000 are serving in the guard and reserve forces where they account for 3.4 percent of the total.

Currently female members of the U.S. armed forces comprise about 14 percent of active-duty personnel. But, in relation to the UCLA study, they comprise more than 43 percent of lesbian, gay or bisexual men and women who are on active duty.

Lifting DADT restrictions could draw an estimated 36,700 men and women to active-duty service and 12,000 more individuals to the guard and reserve, Gates said.

The study calculated that Don't Ask/Don't Tell had cost the military between $290 million and more than half a billion dollars since it was introduced in 1994.

Members of the armed forces discharged under the policy can also incur costs, said the study. According to its current estimates, the military spends between $22,000 and $43,000 per person replaced under DADT.

Sexual Orientation Is Irrelevant to Job Effectiveness

American Psychoanalytic Association

*The American Psychoanalytic Association (ApsaA) is a profes-
sional organization for psychoanalysts that focuses on education
and research of mental health issues.*

The American Psychoanalytic Association (Apsaa) opposes
the military policy mandated by Title 10 of the United
States Code (Section 654) which prohibits an individual's service in the military on the basis of sexual orientation. Section
654 bans openly gay, lesbian and bisexual individuals from
serving in the military. ApsaA strongly advocates that the
United States Government overturn the current policy.

Detrimental Effects of Banning Gays

It is the position of ApsaA that sexual orientation is not germane to any aspect of military effectiveness, including unit
cohesion, morale, recruitment or retention. Empirical evidence, as well as comparative data from foreign militaries and
domestic police and fire departments shows that when lesbians, gay men and bisexuals are allowed to serve openly there
is no evidence of disruption. ApsaA recognizes and abhors the
many detrimental effects the policy has had on individual service members, the military and the United States society since
the enactment of Title 10 section 654 in 1994. Years of psy-
chological research and experience have shown the extensive
mental toll of keeping one's sexual orientation hidden. Man-
dating a ban on self disclosure of sexual orientation for personnel in uniform is thus unnecessarily harmful to their mental health and well being. It also creates ethical dilemmas for
military mental health providers.

Personnel in uniform are currently at war and find the love and support of their families to be essential in supporting them in carrying out their missions. Under the current government policy, lesbian, gay and bisexual military members must be vigilant not to inadvertently disclose their sexual orientation. They are unable to contact their partners and loved ones openly via phone or e-mail when away from home for fear of being discovered. On military forms they cannot list their partners as "next of kin" when they are to be notified in an emergency. At such specific times of distress or emergency, these individuals are isolated and restricted from having equally unguarded and honest access to the support of their loved ones and families.

Integration Can Be Achieved

The U.S. military is capable of integrating members of groups historically excluded from its ranks, as demonstrated by its success in reducing both racial and gender discrimination. Where openly lesbian, gay and bisexual individuals have been allowed to serve in the U.S. Armed Forces there has been no evidence of disruption or loss of mission effectiveness. APsaA thus reaffirms its support for men and women in uniform and its dedication to promoting their health and well being. APsaA endorses the amelioration of the negative effects of the current law through the training and education of mental health professionals and the dissemination of scientific knowledge and professional expertise relevant to implementing this resolution.

The U.S. military is capable of integrating members of groups historically excluded from its ranks.

This statement is part of APsaA's strong ongoing commitment to removing the stigma of mental illness that has long been associated with homosexual, bisexual and transgender behavior and orientations; promoting the health and well-being of lesbian, gay, bisexual and transgender adults and youth; eliminating violence against lesbian, gay, bisexual and transgender armed service members; and working to ensure the equality of lesbian, gay, bisexual and transgender people, both as individuals and members of committed same-sex relationships, in such areas as employment, housing, public accommodation, licensing, parenting and access to legal benefits.

"Don't Ask Don't Tell" Does Not Work

Roger McShane

Roger McShane is the US online editor and frequent blogger for The Economist, *a weekly newspaper focusing on international politics and business news and opinion.*

Today I found myself picking through Mr [William] Kristol's latest *Weekly Standard* editorial, in which he makes the case for maintaining the "don't ask, don't tell" (DADT) policy that allows gays to serve in America's military only if they keep their sexual preference under wraps. Mr Kristol's argument is familiar. It rests on the notion that some soldiers are homophobic and, therefore, any change to the policy might negatively affect morale. Yet he presents little evidence to back up his claim. Because I am startled by his blatant, unsupported, anachronistic bigotry, I thought I might amuse myself by offering up Mr Kristol's article in full, peppered with pointed interjections from myself.

Rebutting Arguments for Keeping DADT

In his State of the Union address, [US president] Barack Obama worried that "too many of our citizens have lost faith" in "our biggest institutions." Many of those institutions have, of course, invited disillusionment with their feckless and irresponsible behavior. But poll after poll shows that at least one major American institution retains citizens' faith. Indeed, this institution has improved its standing in recent years as respect for others has declined. That institution is the U.S. military.

So what institution does the president want to subject to an untested, unnecessary, and probably unwise social experiment? The U.S. military.

Social experiment? Open and peaceful cohabitation with non-heterosexuals is a social experiment that has been going on for decades, with fairly good results. But yes, it is "unnecessary", in the same way that allowing blacks to serve on equal terms was unnecessary, if you happened to be white.

"This year," the president informed us, "I will work with Congress and our military to finally repeal the law that denies gay Americans the right to serve the country they love because of who they are."

It's hard to know where that "finally" came from. Until a year ago, Americans had elected presidents who were in favor of upholding "Don't Ask, Don't Tell"—so if action on this has been overdue, it's only been for the single year of the Obama presidency.

Open and peaceful cohabitation with non-heterosexuals is a social experiment that has been going on for decades, with fairly good results.

The "finally" comes from over five years of polling showing support for repealing the law. Or maybe it was "finally" as in "finally, eight years after beginning one war and six years after starting a second, concurrent one, stretching the forces to the breaking point, we are considering letting all able Americans serve openly."

But the repeal is something that Obama campaigned on. He believes in it.

Wait, not only is he lobbying to make this change, but he also "believes" in it? What an awkward misuse of elected office!

But with all due respect to his sincerely held if abstractly formed views on this subject, it would be reckless to require the military to carry out a major sociological change, one contrary to the preferences of a large majority of its members, as it fights two wars.

"Abstract" is of course a way to dismiss the bookish Mr Obama, as opposed to Mr Kristol, the editor of an opinion magazine. Major sociological change? Isn't that what men complained about when women started wearing trousers? Gays already serve in the military, so clearly they are capable of controlling their animal-like desire for the same sex. As for "the preferences of a large majority" of the military, according to the latest poll I could find, in 2006, 26% of military members agreed with allowing gays and lesbians to serve openly in the military, 32% were neutral and 37% disagreed.

And even if one understood this change to be rectifying an injustice, the fact is it's an injustice that affects perhaps a few thousand people in a nation of 300 million.

Oh, who cares then.

But, "It's the right thing to do," said the president.

Here is contemporary liberalism in a nutshell: No need to consider costs as well as benefits.

Contemporary liberals could learn a thing or two from the neoconservative war on terror, which was amazing for the way it involved an inexpensive pursuit of achievable goals with measurable signs of progress. But Mr Obama gets lucky here, as a repeal of DADT would actually eliminate some unnecessary costs in terms of manpower.

No acknowledgment of competing goods or coexisting rights.

"Coexisting rights"? Does he mean the right to be homophobic? Well, soldiers are in luck: those that hate gay people can keep on hating. In this free country, we are allowed to hate whomever we want.

> No appreciation of the constraints of public sentiment or the challenges of organizational complexity.

Who's not showing an appreciation for public sentiment? As for the challenges of organisational complexity, is it that Mr Kristol believes bigotry is so enmeshed in the bureaucracy of the military that it is just too hard to get rid of it? Regardless, it is always amusing when a conservative suddenly embraces federal bureaucracy [which they are ideologically against] as an argument against reform.

> No sense that not every part of society can be treated dogmatically according to certain simple propositions. Just the assertion that something must be done because it is in some abstract way "the right thing."

Wasn't that the justification for the Iraq war? Mike Mullen, the chairman of the joint chiefs of staff, also says repealing DADT is "the right thing to do". The abstract liberal admiral doesn't think soldiers should have to "lie about who they are in order to defend their fellow citizens".

> [Senator] John McCain's response to Obama's statement was that of a grown-up: "This successful policy has been in effect for over 15 years, and it is well understood and predominantly supported by our military at all levels. We have the best trained, best equipped, and most professional force in the history of our country, and the men and women in uniform are performing heroically in two wars. At a time when our Armed Forces are fighting and sacrificing on the battlefield, now is not the time to abandon the policy."

First of all, John McCain is not the commander in chief, despite all those years spent in pursuit of the top job. So maybe he isn't the best embodiment of the American will. Also, what's with the term "predominant support" again? In the 2006 poll mentioned above, only a little over a third of soldiers were against homosexuals serving openly. And the military's views on the matter have only loosened up since then. In 2008 more than 100 admirals and generals openly called for the repeal of DADT. America's top military leader is calling for it. If our forces are so professional, as Mr McCain claims, you'd think they'd be able to handle fighting next to gay soldiers, who are "performing heroically", "fighting and sacrificing" too.

Being gay doesn't make one less able to perform as a soldier, unless we assume that everyone around them is disruptively homophobic.

Whatever its muddled origins and theoretical deficiencies, the fact is "Don't Ask, Don't Tell" works pretty well at accommodating the complex demands of a war-ready military nestled in a liberal society.

Pretty well, apart from the 12,000 discharges of otherwise able soldiers and the numerous lawsuits. (And again, it's a matter of perspective: Forcing blacks to sit at the back of the bus worked "pretty well" for white people. The discrepancy of incomes between men and women works "pretty well" for men.)

The advocates of repeal say, it's a matter of basic rights. No, it's not. Leave aside the fact that there are difficult and unresolved questions of how our society should deal in various areas of public policy with questions of sexual orientation. There is no basic right to serve in the military. That's why forms of discrimination we would ban in civilian life are permitted: Women have less opportunity to fight than men. The disabled are discriminated against, as are the short, the near-sighted, and the old.

Except homosexuality is not a disability. In the other categories Mr Kristol mentions, people are discriminated against because they have been deemed physically unfit to perform tasks necessary to be a soldier. Being gay doesn't make one less able to perform as a soldier, unless we assume that everyone around them is disruptively homophobic. Luckily, though, Mr Kristol is not representative of the average military man.

> Advocates of repeal will say sexual orientation is irrelevant to military performance in a way these attributes are not. But this is not clearly true given the peculiar characteristics of military service.

What "attributes"? What "peculiar characteristics"? Perhaps military service demands that all sexism be directed towards women?

> We'll hear a lot, as the debate moves forward, about gay Arabic translators being discharged from military service.

What?! Our one Arabic translator may also be gay? Good lord. Maybe God *is* on their side. . . .

> A decision to separate from the military someone who is sitting in an office in Northern Virginia may look silly. But the Obama Defense Department is entirely free to ensure that those men and women continue to use their skills to serve their country in those same offices as civilians.

Wait, so they'd be given separate jobs, but equal ones. Have I got that right? ["Separate but equal" was the motto of racial segregationists.]

> And translators who are uniformed members of the military are subject to the usual demands of training and deployment, so the questions about the effect of open homosexuals on unit morale and cohesion in training and combat situations remain relevant.

Clearly Mr Kristol's imagination is running away with him. As for these relevant questions about the effect of open homosexuality on "unit morale and cohesion", Mr Kristol offers no answers, only the projection of disruptive homophobia. Robert Gates, the defence secretary, has planned a review of DADT, which will surely study morale and cohesion issues. That sounds like a more grown-up response.

> As an intellectual matter, gays in the military is a not uninteresting question. We have our views, as does President Obama, and we are not averse to debating the issue. But surely there are more pressing and important matters for our political and military leaders to be spending their time on.

And there always will be, in Mr Kristol's view.

Gay Rights Should Not
Take Precedence over
Service Members' Privacy

Paul Benedict

Paul Benedict is a teacher from California with libertarian views who writes a column on Nolan Chart, a website that provides a platform for people to express their political views.

We all know a straight guy on a three month submarine tour would rather hot bunk with a co-ed, but for the glory of his country or the promise of seeing the world, he's taken a deal he doesn't like much: he's bunking, in shifts, with dozens of smelly guys he'd rather only play poker with. As folks grow older and wiser, they look back and can't even understand how they managed to live with their fraternity brothers in the "good old days." This resiliency of youth should be guarded and protected. This resiliency, the ability to live as brethren with those who are nearly strangers, is, among other things, an ability to ignore sexuality. Those that want gay rights in the military would force sexuality into every inch of these dormitories of patriotic celibacy. However, we are to believe their motives are selfless, kind, caring and good. I guess gay rights are more important than the rights of our young patriots to the last vestiges of their personal privacy.

Ignoring Sexuality

Homosexuality is about sexuality. The *esprit d'corps* critical to military service, especially where heterosexual men and women serve together, is about ignoring sexuality. There is no reason for it to be a "gay right" to inject sexuality into that mix. If it is a need for individual homosexuals to do this, they shouldn't serve. This is as it is for heterosexuals as well. Heterosexuals who cannot contain themselves, who must overtly express sexual intentions in the workplace, end up out of today's military also. The sacrifice of our youth in the service of our nation is heroic enough. Their unit cohesion depends on brotherhood and trust. That brotherhood (and, where applicable, sisterhood) depends, to a great extent, on the ability to overcome the need to make overt one's sexuality and sexual intentions. Making "gay rights" an issue by injecting sexuality into dormitories, showers, and foxholes is not in the best interests of the military.

There are many areas of life and society in which America willingly chooses to help those who are, in any way, limited by the conditions of birth or nature. We willingly place wheel chair ramps for the handicapped and provide brail [sic] for the blind in public education. We are a kind and magnanimous people. We consider the effects of poverty on educational development and seek to compensate so that the playing field is level for all. We even allow for mental disease to mitigate in our judgments of criminal offenses. However, in the military and in emergency services, ability, and only ability, should be the criteria for service. Weakness, whether heterosexual or homosexual, should not be enshrined in the military codes as "protected" in any way.

Making "gay rights" an issue by injecting sexuality into dormitories, showers, and foxholes is not in the best interests of the military.

A domestic partner is not the same thing as a spouse. If an entire branch of government wants to open up the flood gates of the "government treasury" (what's the national debt—15 trillion?) and allow people to freely sign up for benefits with any single friend they know, the tax payers have a right to know about it and vote on it. It is a matter of somebody's rights. It is a matter of the right of taxpayers to their property.

Nor is demanding gays openly serve in the military like integrating blacks and whites. To insist that it is, is racist. Insisting on such an analogy, when the comparison is unmasked and shown for what it is, is to say that being black is a disability that runs contrary to the evolutionary natural design of mankind. Hitler would love you.

Open Service for Gays Promotes Gay Rights, Not Military Strength

Bill Murchison

Bill Murchison is an author and senior columnist for The Dallas Morning News, *a Texas newspaper.*

The motive behind the proposed repeal of the military's "don't ask, don't tell" policy is, hmmm . . . what, exactly?

A stronger military? Better projection of American might in tight corners like Afghanistan and South Korea?

Well, not precisely any of that. The whole idea of opening military enlistment to professed gays is the furtherance of the gay rights cause. It is what you might call an odd motive indeed for adoption of a military policy with mainly cultural implications.

Unknown Impacts

That Congress has no clear idea how such a policy would work seems not to matter to its liberal promoters, clustered behind shoulder-boarded military brass who say with varying degrees of confidence and enthusiasm, yes, the thing can be done. Can be done isn't—alas—the same thing as ought to be done: least of all in a time of war.

Defense Secretary Robert Gates, in Senate Armed Services Committee hearings, did not stunningly reassure Sen. John McCain, a third generation Naval man known to have acquired some insights into the ways of fighting men.

Gates was brandishing poll results purporting to show that 70 percent of military personnel thought that the insertion of gays into military units could likely work out. Oh? said McCain. What about the 58 percent of Marines and 48 percent of Army personnel otherwise minded?

"With time and adequate preparation," said Gates, "we can mitigate their concerns."

"Well, I couldn't disagree more," said McCain: pulling, if you like, moral rank.

Adm. Michael Mullen, chairman of the Joint Chiefs of Staff, was no more persuasive than Gates. He noted that, yes, particular heterosexuals in the service might have a hard time with repeal of "don't ask, don't tell." "Some may ask for different berthing," he related. "Some may even quit the service."

Nobody . . . knows explicitly how matters might work out should gays be incorporated freely and openly into the ranks.

With what net gain for the military, and for the security Americans claim as an entitlement? As it happens, that's the $64 trillion question: to which no bureaucrat or politician has an uncomplicated answer. For the sake of furthering an essentially political cause, Congress and the president are invited to throw open barrack gates to advocates for a political cause not guaranteed, shall we say, to perfect unity in battle.

Well, now, as everybody presumably knows, gays in the barracks wouldn't be an innovation. The military has always had such—the difference between yesterday and today being, their presence in military units was inadvertent; when it was discovered, expulsion followed. Then gayness became a cause—a standard for rallying around. Whether the military needs explicit advocates for a cultural cause is the question McCain has tried to broach, with minimal cooperation from the military bureaucrats who work for President Obama.

Nobody—Gates, Mullen or McCain—knows explicitly how matters might work out should gays be incorporated freely and openly into the ranks. That is the point—nobody knows. Inferences nevertheless abound. What if McCain's suspicions are correct, and sexual tensions—a potent enough factor with women now in the ranks—cause dissension, putting lives in danger? Are we willing to take that chance? If so, why?

Racial integration of the services following World War II was a different kettle of fish. For one thing, sex normally outranks race as a self-identifier. For another, black and white units already existed side by side; President Truman, in 1948, merely ordered their merger. A third difference: the country was at peace, and relatively unified, at the time of the merger.

This whole business after all isn't about a stronger, better military. The drive to repeal "don't ask, don't tell" is about political promises to the gay rights movement.

Well, the liberal response is so what, in spirit if not words, to civilized objections such as McCain raises to taking chances with military security. This whole business after all isn't about a stronger, better military. The drive to repeal "don't ask, don't tell" is about political promises to the gay rights movement and the urgency, as liberals see it, of keeping their base happy and voting liberal. Just what the country needs right now—political and cultural warfare over who fights our wars and on what terms.

Repealing "Don't Ask Don't Tell" Will Disregard Some Military Members' Religious Beliefs

Ethics & Religious Liberty Commission

The Ethics & Religious Liberty Commission is an entity of the Southern Baptist Convention, the largest Protestant denomination in the country. The commission is dedicated to addressing social and moral concerns and their implications for public policy.

Southern Baptist ethicist Richard Land has joined other conservative leaders in calling for a congressional effort to protect the U.S. military as repeal of the ban on open homosexuality in the Armed Forces nears implementation.

President [Barack] Obama signed into law in December [2010] legislation repealing the Don't Ask, Don't Tell law. Final revocation of the policy, however, will not take effect until Obama, Secretary of Defense Robert Gates and Joint Chiefs of Staff Chairman Michael Mullen certify the reversal will not harm the military. That seems to be a given, since all three supported the bill. Even then, a 60-day waiting period is required until the new policy becomes effective.

Still Time to Save Our Military

In a letter to Republican leaders of the House of Representatives Armed Services Committee, Land and other members of the Freedom Federation coalition said, "[T]here is still time to save our military, and especially our service members with sincerely held religious beliefs that will, inevitably, be silenced by nondiscrimination policies that elevate and favor sexual minorities."

Land is president of the Ethics & Religious Liberty Commission.

The coalition urged Reps. Buck McKeon, R.-Calif., the committee's chairman, and Joe Wilson, R.-S.C., the Military Personnel Subcommittee's chairman, to hold hearings regarding what they described as "flaws" in the Pentagon report on overturning Don't Ask, Don't Tell, as well as the "negative effects of a full repeal" on military effectiveness.

The letter's 32 signers also called for the congressmen to promote a vote on the Restore Military Readiness Act, H.R. 337, which would amend the repeal measure enacted in December. That bill, sponsored by Rep. Duncan Hunter, R.-Calif., would require that—in addition to Obama, Gates and Mullen—each military chief of staff be required to certify that repeal of Don't Ask, Don't Tell will not undermine his branch's combat readiness and effectiveness. Some of the military chiefs did not support the repeal.

Repeal [of Don't Ask Don't Tell] would marginalize "deeply held" religious beliefs of military personnel.

Other signers of the Feb. 3 letter included Mathew Staver, Freedom Foundation's chairman and dean of the Liberty University School of Law; Elaine Donnelly, president of the Center for Military Readiness; Gary Bauer, president of American Values; Penny Nance, chief executive officer of Concerned Women for America; Tom McClusky, senior vice president of Family Research Council Action, and Tom Minnery, senior vice president of CitizenLink.

Don't Ask, Don't Tell—enacted in 1993—barred homosexuals from serving openly in the military but also prohibited commanders from asking service members if they are homosexual or about their "sexual orientation."

Congress' December approval of the repeal proposal occurred during a lame-duck session. The Senate voted 65-31 for repeal, while the House roll call was 250-175 in favor.

Land appealed to Obama in a December letter not to sign the repeal measure, urging him to be guided by his Christian faith. After the signing ceremony, Land described it as a "very, very sad day for America" and expressed concern the change would "significantly degrade" military effectiveness.

[The Pentagon's] survey of military personnel found significant resistance to a reversal [of Don't Ask Don't Tell] from those serving on the front lines.

Objections to Repeal

Opponents of repeal especially expressed concern about religious liberty protections. More than 60 retired chaplains had signed a letter to Obama and Gates warning that a repeal would marginalize "deeply held", religious beliefs of military personnel and present a conflict when some chaplains, while preaching, "present religious teachings that identify homosexual behavior as immoral." They warned that changing the policy could influence chaplains not only in what they could preach but in what they could say in a counseling session.

Though the Pentagon said its study showed that a repeal's risks to the military would be low, its survey of military personnel found significant resistance to a reversal from those serving on the front lines for example, among those in the Marine combat arms and Army combat arms, 57 percent and 47 percent, respectively, said having an openly homosexual person would negatively impact "how service members in your immediate unit work together to get the job done."

More than a third of Marines (38.1 percent) and nearly a fourth of all personnel (23.7) said they would either leave the military or think about doing so earlier than planned if the policy is reversed. That number jumped to 48 percent for Marines on the front lines.

Now Is Not the Time to End "Don't Ask Don't Tell"

William Kristol

William Kristol is editor of The Weekly Standard, *a weekly political magazine featuring conservative views.*

In his [2010] State of the Union address, [US president] Barack Obama worried that "too many of our citizens have lost faith" in "our biggest institutions." Many of those institutions have, of course, invited disillusionment with their feckless and irresponsible behavior. But poll after poll shows that at least one major American institution retains citizens' faith. Indeed, this institution has improved its standing in recent years as respect for others has declined. That institution is the U.S. military.

So what institution does the president want to subject to an untested, unnecessary, and probably unwise social experiment? The U.S. military.

"This year," the president informed us, "I will work with Congress and our military to finally repeal the law that denies gay Americans the right to serve the country they love because of who they are."

The Right Thing?

It's hard to know where that "finally" came from. Until a year ago, Americans had elected presidents who were in favor of upholding "Don't Ask, Don't Tell"—so if action on this has been overdue, it's only been for the single year of the Obama presidency.

But the repeal is something that Obama campaigned on. He believes in it. But with all due respect to his sincerely held if abstractly formed views on this subject, it would be reckless to require the military to carry out a major sociological change, one contrary to the preferences of a large majority of its members, as it fights two wars. What's more, it isn't a change an appreciable number of Americans are clamoring for. And even if one understood this change to be rectifying an injustice, the fact is it's an injustice that affects perhaps a few thousand people in a nation of 300 million.

It would be reckless to require the military to carry out a major sociological change, one contrary to the preferences of a large majority of its members, as it fights two wars.

But, "It's the right thing to do," said the president.

Here is contemporary liberalism in a nutshell: No need to consider costs as well as benefits. No acknowledgment of competing goods or coexisting rights. No appreciation of the constraints of public sentiment or the challenges of organizational complexity. No sense that not every part of society can be treated dogmatically according to certain simple propositions. Just the assertion that something must be done because it is in some abstract way "the right thing."

A Grown-Up View

[Senator] John McCain's response to Obama's statement was that of a grown-up: "This successful policy has been in effect for over 15 years, and it is well understood and predominantly supported by our military at all levels. We have the best trained, best equipped, and most professional force in the history of our country, and the men and women in uniform are performing heroically in two wars. At a time when our Armed Forces are fighting and sacrificing on the battlefield, now is not the time to abandon the policy." Whatever its muddled origins and theoretical deficiencies, the fact is "Don't Ask,

Don't Tell" works pretty well at accommodating the complex demands of a war-ready military nestled in a liberal society.

The advocates of repeal say, it's a matter of basic rights. No, it's not. Leave aside the fact that there are difficult and unresolved questions of how our society should deal in various areas of public policy with questions of sexual orientation. There is no basic right to serve in the military. That's why forms of discrimination we would ban in civilian life are permitted: Women have less opportunity to fight than men. The disabled are discriminated against, as are the short, the near-sighted, and the old.

"Don't Ask, Don't Tell" works pretty well at accommodating the complex demands of a war-ready military nestled in a liberal society.

Advocates of repeal will say sexual orientation is irrelevant to military performance in a way these attributes are not. But this is not clearly true given the peculiar characteristics of military service.

We'll hear a lot, as the debate moves forward, about gay Arabic translators being discharged from military service. A decision to separate from the military someone who is sitting in an office in Northern Virginia may look silly. But the Obama Defense Department is entirely free to ensure that those men and women continue to use their skills to serve their country in those same offices as civilians. And translators who are uniformed members of the military are subject to the usual demands of training and deployment, so the questions about the effect of open homosexuals on unit morale and cohesion in training and combat situations remain relevant.

As an intellectual matter, gays in the military is a not uninteresting question. We have our views, as does President Obama, and we are not averse to debating the issue. But surely there are more pressing and important matters for our political and military leaders to be spending their time on.

Chapter 2

Will Repeal of "Don't Ask Don't Tell" Harm the US Military?

Chapter Preface

The issue of gays serving openly in the military is still a contentious one in the United States, even after the US Congress passed a law in December 2010 repealing the "Don't Ask Don't Tell" policy, allowing gays to serve openly for the first time in US military history. In many foreign countries, however, the matter has long been resolved. In fact, according to the Palm Center, a University of California think tank, twenty-five nations allowed military service by openly gay people as of June 2009. And a November 2010 Pentagon study of the issue identified thirty-five nations that allowed gay service. Among these countries are most of America's allies and the majority of the North Atlantic Treaty Organization (NATO) countries, including Canada, America's closest neighbor, and European countries such as the United Kingdom, France, Spain, Germany, and Italy. Even Israel's military, considered by many to be one of the world's best, allows gays to serve openly. The implementation of the "Don't Ask Don't Tell" repeal, therefore, finally allows the United States to join many other industrialized nations who have liberalized their policies on gay service members.

Altogether, the Palm Center's list of countries that allow openly gay military service is as follows: Australia, Austria, Belgium, Canada, Czech Republic, Denmark, Estonia, Finland, France, Germany, Ireland, Israel, Italy, Lithuania, Luxembourg, The Netherlands, New Zealand, Norway, Slovenia, South Africa, Spain, Sweden, Switzerland, United Kingdom, Uruguay. The Pentagon list, compiled from a review of forty-three NATO and International Security Assistance Force (ISAF)—a group of countries conducting military operations in Afghanistan—adds Albania, Azerbaijan, Bosnia & Herzegovina, Croatia, Georgia, Greece, Hungary, Iceland, Latvia, Portugal, Republic of Korea, Romania, Slovakia, and Ukraine but does not include Slovenia, South Africa, or Uruguay. According to the Pentagon report, only six nations out of the forty-three reviewed—Bulgaria, Jordan, Poland, Turkey, the United Arab Emirates, and the United States (as of November 2010)—excluded gay men and lesbians from serving or serving openly in the military by policy.

According to Aaron Belkin, a political science professor at the University of California–Santa Barbara, most of the countries that allow openly gay military service have had few problems with the policy, and no issues with unit cohesion or military effectiveness. The British military began allowing gays in 2000, for example, and in 2007 Britain's Defense Ministry reported that there had been no incidents of harassment, discord among the troops, or decrease in cohesiveness or effectiveness. Professor Belkin also studied Canada's 1991 transition to allowing openly gay military service, concluding that that nation experienced no changes in military performance, unit cohesion, or discipline.

The countries that explicitly prohibit gays from serving in the military tend to be located in very conservative parts of the world where people have strong religious or cultural objections to homosexuality in general. Much of the Muslim world, for example, and many places in Africa, Asia, and Latin America fit this profile. In fact, there are reportedly about eighty countries in the world that still classify homosexuality as a crime, and in some countries it is even punished by death. Even Russia, a relatively developed and modernized nation, has issues with gay military service—on the one hand considering deviations of gender identification and sexual preferences to be a type of disability preventing military service, but on the other permitting physically and psychologically healthy homosexuals to serve in the Russian military.

The many examples of countries with liberal gay military service policies are often touted by gay advocates in the United States, but some critics say that experiences of other countries are not relevant to whether the US military will be negatively affected by a pro-gay policy. Britain and other countries in Europe, they say, have much smaller militaries than the United States does and much more permissive cultures. Similarly, Israel's military culture differs greatly from that of the US military; Israel, for example, requires universal conscription for both men and women and tolerates dating and relationships within its military, whereas the US military prohibits sexual relationships among service members. According to critics, politicians should not be forcing liberal social policies on the military since no one knows for sure what the impact might be, particularly because many US service members are both conservative and religious. Gay military veterans counter, however, that it's only the older military commanders who have a problem with gay soldiers; the majority of younger recruits, they claim, are much more accepting of people with different sexual preferences. Gay advocates conclude that the military will successfully implement the new gay military policy without major problems just as it did racial and gender integration.

The authors of viewpoints in this chapter address the basic issue of whether gays should serve openly in the US military. The viewpoints include differing views on issues such as whether openly gay service will reduce military effectiveness, whether gays will disrupt cohesion in combat situations, and whether gay rights will advance the military's overall mission.

The Presence of Openly Gay Men in the Military Will Disrupt Unit Cohesion and Morale

Brian Jones

Brian Jones is a retired US Army sergeant major who served for twenty-one years in the Rangers and special operations, including a six-month deployment in Iraq. He is currently the chief executive officer of Adventure Training Concepts, a company that provides teamwork training to civilians using the US Army training model.

I am a retired Sergeant Major, US Army. I am a Ranger first and always. The most common attribute that I see on Military evaluation reports is "selfless service". I chose a career path that placed me in a Ranger Battalion, Delta Force, and as a Detachment Sergeant Major at the Ranger Regiment.

Selfless service is what makes a good team great within the US Military. You won't find that, in truth, in the corporate world. Selfless Service is what an individual will do for the good of the team; self-service is doing what is in a personal self interest, at the expense of the team. Recently, a US Navy SEAL received the Congressional Medal of Honor by throwing himself on a grenade to protect his team. That is selfless service.

While deployed to Somalia in 1993, commonly referred to as "Blackhawk Down", two of our unit members received the Medal of Honor for asking to be inserted into a crash site to protect a pilot, knowing what their fate would be. That is self-

Brian Jones, "Statement of Brian Jones, Sergeant Major USA (Ret) CEO, Adventure Training Concepts, House Armed Services Committee, Subcommittee on Personnel, In Support of Section 654, Title 10, the 1993 Law Stating that Homosexuals Are Not Eligible to Serve in the Military," CMRlink.org, July 23, 2008. Copyright © 2008 by Center for Military Readiness. All rights reserved. Reproduced by permission of the author.

less service, and combat effectiveness depends on it. It does not happen by accident—it must be taught with concentrated training—no distractions. Selfless service is reinforced with discipline, and encouraged by the example of combat leaders.

The Military World

The Ranger way of life trained me for what I do now as the CEO of a company I started three years ago, Adventure Training Concepts [ATC]. The concept of ATC is to use the US Army training model to teach the value of teamwork during Corporate Team Building and Leadership Development Training.

Our clients are diverse—men and women, adventure seekers of all ages and, I suspect, some who are homosexual. All of them enjoy and benefit professionally from the lessons in teamwork taught by ATC programs. There is a notable difference, however, between the ATC environment and military units such as the infantry, special operations forces, and submarines. On my facility, people learn about teamwork and leadership for 6 hours over a couple of days, but they do not share close, intimate living conditions comparable to those in the military. The difference is critically important and disregarded at great risk.

In the military environment, team cohesion, morale, and esprit de corps is a matter of life and death.

In the civilian business world, decisions frequently are based on bonuses and job security. In the military environment, team cohesion, morale, and esprit de corps is a matter of life and death. Bonus and job security come second to the reality of writing the hard letter to a loved one, or holding the hand of a teammate who is fighting for his or her life.

In my 21 years of service in the US Army, I sought, and performed in as many leadership positions that I could. As a leader, my first obligation was to the Nation. It meant keeping our soldiers ready for any situation for which our country called upon them. It meant taking care of each soldier I had the honor of leading. It meant being fair and impartial to every soldier. It also meant keeping the soldiers under my charge as safe, secure, trained, equipped, and informed as I possibly could.

> It is difficult to understand why a minority faction is demanding that their concerns be given priority over more important issues.

On their behalf, I would respectfully like to say that in this time of war, I find it surprising that we are here today to talk about this issue of repealing the 1993 law. Our soldiers are over-tasked with deploying, fighting, redeploying, refitting, and deploying again. These brave men and women have achieved what many Americans thought impossible. With all of the important issues that require attention, it is difficult to understand why a minority faction is demanding that their concerns be given priority over more important issues.

As a US Army Ranger, I performed long-range patrols in severe cold weather conditions, in teams of 10, with only mission essential items on our backs. No comfort items. The only way to keep from freezing at night was to get as close as possible for body heat—which means skin to skin. On several occasions, in the close quarters that a team lives, any attraction to same sex teammates, real or perceived, would be known and would be a problem. The presence of openly gay men in these situations would elevate tensions and disrupt unit cohesion and morale.

No Comparison to Foreign Militaries

I have served alongside many foreign militaries. None of them compares to the US Military. In every case, they would give anything to be like ours. Lack of discipline, morale, and values top the list of reasons why. Between 1997 and 2001 I worked with Armies from Poland, Italy, England, and France. The discipline, training, and core values are quite different. Here are two specific examples:

- Operation Deep Strike, 1999, 1st deployment exercise into Poland. I personally had to take charge of a Logistical Transfer point inside Poland when I stopped there (as a [sergeant major]) and was horrified at what was going on at this Polish Infantry base. The Captain (US) in charge displayed incompetence and poor judgment when, he placed the females in the Polish infantry barracks. The females were absolutely traumatized. They were surrounded by Polish Infantry in the shower, heckled and harassed constantly. I had to control my outrage while giving this Captain a lecture on "common sense". My point is that the culture of the Polish military force was very different from the high standards in ours.

- 2004, Tallil, Iraq. Similar to the Polish Army, the Italian Army occupied a compound at Tallil, Iraq. Again, drinking during deployment is the norm for them. The Italians would lay in wait at the PX [military store], and target females, inviting them to their "bunker" on the Italian compound. There were so many incidents of rape, harassment, and sexual misconduct reported, that the Italian compound had to be placed "OFF LIMITS". This did not stop further incidents; the Italians always seemed to be one step ahead. Again, the culture, discipline, and leadership of the Italian military is different from ours. I am not a diplomat, and I hope you do not mind my saying this. My concern is our military—the men and women who courageously volunteer to serve.

As an American soldier, I can't imagine comparing our Military to that of a foreign nation to justify a change in policy. We should be very proud of the fact that they would rather be like us. Let's keep it that way.

Repealing the 1993 law will not help us win this war on terrorism or any conflict that our military is called upon to fight and win in the future. Too much time is being spent on how we can hinder our great men and women in the military, let's do what we can to lift their morale, give them more resolve, and motivate them to continue the absolutely great job that they are doing. I hope that this Congress will not make their jobs more difficult and dangerous than they already are by repealing a solid law that continues to support the morale, discipline, and readiness of our troops.

Combat Troops Will Be Weakened by the Repeal of "Don't Ask Don't Tell"

Elaine Donnelly

Elaine Donnelly is president of the Center for Military Readiness, an independent, nonpartisan public policy organization that specializes in military/social issues.

On Saturday [December 18, 2010,] the United States Senate voted for legislation that will impose heavy, unnecessary burdens on the backs of military men and women. They are the ones who will pay a very high price for Congress' reckless decision to help President Barack Obama deliver on political campaign promises to LGBT (lesbian, gay, bisexual, transgender) activists.

Sixty-five senators voted for the no-amendments-allowed "privileged" bill in a lame-duck session. History will note that the outgoing 111th Congress acted with needless haste allowing no time for substantive hearings to examine findings and controversial recommendations in the Pentagon's Comprehensive Review Working Group [CRWG] Report.

Liberals in Congress knew that the report could not withstand informed scrutiny, so Sen. Susan Collins (R-ME) persuaded others to join her in breaking their word on legislative priorities—a betrayal that belied her own previous statements calling for full and open debate. Full hearings and informed oversight probably would have halted this controversial bill.

Adding insult to grievous and possibly irreversible injury, Sen. Joe Lieberman (I-CT) celebrated "victory" for his legislation by praising the results of First Amendment rights enjoyed by well-funded, mostly-civilian LGBT Left groups. The remark was a thoughtless affront to concerned combat troops who tried to express support for the current law through the Pentagon's Working Group process.

Loss of Valuable Troops

Without providing quantitative data on the results of focus groups nationwide and overseas, the Working Group conceded, "Our sense is that the majority of views expressed were against repeal." Not only were these opinions disrespected, [Joint Chiefs chairman] Adm. Mike Mullen has already stated more than once that anyone who disagrees with the LGBT law no longer will be welcome to serve.

Among Army combat arms personnel, 21.4% would leave sooner than planned, and 14.6% would think about leaving—a total potential loss of more than a third (36%) of those valuable troops.

In addition to involuntary personnel losses due to Adm. Mullen's "zero tolerance" of dissent, cross-tabbed data displayed on the 2010 DADT [Don't Ask Don't Tell] Survey website indicate that among Army combat arms personnel, 21.4% would leave sooner than planned, and 14.6% would think about leaving—a total potential loss of more than a third (36%) of those valuable troops.

Marine combat arms would be weakened even more, with 32% of Marines saying they would leave sooner than planned, and 16.2% considering an early end to their careers, totaling almost half. The gradual loss of so many combat troops and what the report described as "only 12%" of families likely to decline re-enlistment could put remaining troops in greater danger, and *break* the All-Volunteer Force.

Such findings should make it impossible for President Barack Obama, Defense Secretary Robert Gates and Joint

Chiefs Chairman Adm. Mike Mullen to "certify" that no harm will be done by implementation of their own plans for repeal. The president's political promise to LGBT Left groups has been assigned highest priority, at the expense of Army and Marine combat troops whose voices were heard but ignored.

Marine combat arms would be weakened even more, with 32% of Marines saying they would leave sooner than planned, and 16.2% considering an early end to their careers, totaling almost half.

Senator James Webb (D-VA), who rationalized his vote by relying on such a promise from Secretary Gates, has played the same role that Rep. Bart Stupak (D-MI) did when he accepted worthless assurances from the administration in exchange for his vote on the health care bill.

The Real Meaning of DADT Repeal

Some media commentators are asking—belatedly—what repeal of the 1993 law would mean. All should consider the self-inflicted problems presaged in the CRWG Report, and proposed "mitigation" strategies advocated in the Support Plan for Implementation. To mention only a few, they include:

- A mandate to "prohibit the creation of separate bath-room and shower facilities based on sexual orientation." Such a policy, tantamount to forced cohabitation of men with military women, would disregard normal dynamics of human sexuality. Local commanders dealing with unprecedented problems would be, essentially, on their own.

- Mandatory "three-tiered" education program, focusing on resistant combat troops, to change attitudes and opinions on LGBT issues. The plan does not suggest ways to get personnel accustomed to routine personal exposure to others who may be sexually attracted to them, in conditions of "forced intimacy" offering little or no privacy.

- Punishments for "resistance;" i.e., zero tolerance of anyone who disagrees for any reason, including "moral or religious beliefs." Senate testimony confirmed that an undetermined number of chaplains having moral conflicts with LGBT policies would be lost to the service. The report concedes that on the issue of religious freedom for chaplains, "boundaries are not always clearly defined." Litigation is guaranteed, but Congress has surrendered decision-making power to unelected bureaucrats or federal courts.

- Repeal of certain personal conduct provisions in the UCMJ [Uniform Code of Military Justice], eliminating or lowering some standards to accommodate consensual homosexual conduct. Congress has just voted to repeal statutory findings that rules of conduct apply both on- and off-base.

- Unresolved issues involving marital status, including disparities in benefits and access to family medical care in states that do not recognize same-sex marriages, plus access to military family housing for opposite- and same-sex unmarried couples. Again, the courts will likely decide, at the behest of administration, who will cite LGBT Law in the military to accomplish repeal of the DOMA [Defense of Marriage Act].

- Unresolved questions about morale and costs related to the retention of HIV+ personnel, who must be retained in non-deployable status under current regulations.

A thorough reading of the entire report and its recommendations reveals not a single point or argument showing consequences that would *benefit* the All-Volunteer Force. Instead, the document recommends "mitigation" of expected problems, and downplays risks by making the absurd claim that all will go smoothly if the Working Group's recommendations are followed, no matter how unrealistic or potentially harmful they are.

The elitism and arrogance behind these flawed recommendations will cause years of harmful consequences, which our troops did nothing to deserve. History will hold accountable every legislator who voted to make it happen.

A Gay Agenda for the US Military Does Not Advance the Armed Forces' Mission

Tony Perkins

Tony Perkins is president of Family Research Group, a conservative advocacy organization that promotes faith, family, and freedom issues in public policy and public opinion.

The order from the Commander in Chief to the nation's military last month [January 2010] in his first State of the Union Address was clear—embrace the gay agenda. This command from on high is troubling to me, not just in my capacity as the head of a national organization working to preserve and promote family values, but as a veteran of the United States Marine Corps.

There's no question that allowing active, self-professed homosexuals to serve openly in the military would advance the political and social agenda not only in the military but in public, including gay marriage.

However, our armed forces do not exist to advance a narrow political, social, or cultural agenda. They exist to keep our country safe by being prepared to fight and win wars. What has changed since this compromise policy was adopted 16 years ago? Maybe the fact that we are now involved in two wars and face the constant threat of terrorist attacks?

In light of these changes the question that I urge Congress to ask, and those pushing this change to answer is how will recruiting of homosexuals serve the needs of the military, helping them better accomplishing their mission of keeping America safe.

Retention Concerns

The military's longstanding prohibition on homosexual conduct dates all the way back to George Washington's Continental Army, not just to the current law passed in 1993. There is no reason to believe repealing that law would increase the military's effectiveness, and there are several ways it could reduce it. Like a grade school lesson, we can summarize these issues in terms of "the three R's" for the military—recruiting, readiness, and retention.

Our armed forces do not exist to advance a narrow political, social, or cultural agenda. They exist to keep our country safe by being prepared to fight and win wars.

Let's look at these in reverse order, beginning with retention. Advocates for allowing homosexuality in the military argue that the military could not afford to lose the talents of the estimated 13,000 individuals who have been separated from the service in accordance with the terms of the 1993 law. However, those discharges represent only a tiny percentage of all those discharged from active duty during the same period.

During the most recent ten years, the 8,336 people discharged for homosexuality represented less than one half of one percent of the 1.9 *million* separated from active duty during that period—despite the fact that our nation was fighting two wars for much of that time. And many of those people were discharged for reasons that would not be accepted as valid for most civilian employers, such as obesity or pregnancy.

On the other hand, we must consider the likelihood that many current service members would be reluctant to serve with open homosexuals, and choose to leave voluntarily. A survey in the *Military Times* showed that ten percent of currently serving personnel would leave if the military were opened to homosexuals, and another fourteen percent would consider leaving. These figures dwarf the tiny number of homosexuals who have been discharged in recent years.

Readiness Issues

Furthermore, the concerns of our soldiers about a gay military are not based on irrational prejudice, but on legitimate worries about the consequences of increased sexual tension, sexual harassment, and even sexual assault on morale and unit cohesion. Such problems in turn would threaten the readiness of the force. Can we really casually dismiss the reluctance of soldiers to endure forced cohabitation with those who may view them as a sexual object? If so, would we be prepared to force the same upon our female soldiers?

The concerns of our soldiers about a gay military are not based on irrational prejudice, but on legitimate worries about the consequences . . . on morale and unit cohesion.

There would also be more specific threats to readiness. People who are HIV-positive are not permitted to enlist in the military. But if someone on active duty becomes infected, they cannot be deployed in combat—yet current policy also forbids them from being discharged. Since scientists have said that homosexuals and bisexuals are fifty times more likely to contract HIV, it is inevitable that welcoming them into the military will increase both medical costs and the number of personnel who are essentially dead weight within the force.

Recruiting Problems

Finally, what would be the impact on recruiting? The idea that the military simply cannot get by without recruiting among the tiny fraction (about two percent) of the population who are homosexual is simply a myth. In recent years, the armed services have been meeting or exceeding their recruiting goals.

While no segment of American society has a monopoly on courage or patriotism, it would be naïve to ignore the fact that more conservative families are disproportionately likely to send their sons and daughters into military service. But they are the most likely to be discouraged from doing so if an agenda of political correctness and sexual freedom comes to trump the warrior culture of discipline and honor. Indeed, such a change could break the back of the all-volunteer force—leaving no choice but a return to the draft in order to meet military manpower needs.

Homosexuality is incompatible with military service.

Some people argue that the law should change because society has changed. But the unique mission, needs, and culture of the military have not. Studying the "three R's" of the military leads to one conclusion—homosexuality is incompatible with military service. Our armed forces do not exist to serve the needs of a single interest group, but to protect and defend this nation and all our people. That's a bottom line too important to ignore.

Research Shows That Openly Gay Service Does Not Reduce Military Cohesion

Nathaniel Frank

Nathaniel Frank is an adjunct professor of history at New York University and a senior research fellow at the Palm Center, a research institute located at the University of California–Santa Barbara. He also is a writer, blogger, and author of the 2009 book Unfriendly Fire: How the Gay Ban Undermines the Military and Weakens America.

Research on openly gay service is extensive, and includes over half a century of evidence gathered by independent researchers and the U.S. military itself, as well as the study of the experience of foreign militaries. The U.S. military's own researchers have consistently found that openly gay service does not undermine cohesion, and the military has repeatedly sought to condemn or suppress these conclusions when they emerged. Yet no research has ever shown that open homosexuality impairs military readiness. This fact has been acknowledged by the Government Accountability Office and by the Pentagon, which has said in response to evidence suggesting that openly gay service works that its policy is "inherently subjective in nature" and is the result of "professional Military judgment, not scientific or sociological analysis." Below are the major research studies on service by gays and lesbians.

Nathaniel Frank, "What Does the Empirical Research Say About the Impact of Openly Gay Service on the Military? A Research Memo," The Palm Center, March 3, 2010. www.PalmCenter.org. Copyright © 2010 by The Palm Center. All rights reserved. Reproduced by permission.

1. In 1957, the secretary of the navy appointed a panel to investigate its homosexual exclusion policy. The outcome, known as the Crittenden report, stated that "the number of cases of blackmail as a result of past investigations of homosexuals is negligible" and "no factual data exist to support the contention that homosexuals are a greater risk than heterosexuals."

2. In 1988, the Personnel Security Research and Education Center (PERSEREC) commissioned studies that found no evidence showing that gays were unsuitable for military service and suggested that the policy was unnecessary and damaging. The first report pointed to growing tolerance of homosexuality and concluded that "the military cannot indefinitely isolate itself from the changes occurring in the wider society, of which it is an integral part." It found that "having a same-gender or an opposite gender orientation is unrelated to job performance in the same way as being left- or right-handed." The second report found that "the preponderance of the evidence presented indicates that homosexuals show pre-service suitability-related adjustment that is as good [as] or better than the average heterosexual," a result that appeared to "conflict with conceptions of homosexuals as unstable, maladjusted persons."

3. In 1992, the Government Accountability Office (GAO) conducted its own study of the gay exclusion policy. Its researchers looked at seventeen different countries and eight police and fire departments in four U.S. cities and reviewed military and nonmilitary polls, studies, legal decisions, and scholarly research on homosexual service. The GAO recommended in an early draft that Congress "may wish to direct the Secretary of Defense to reconsider the basis" for gay exclusion.

4. In 1993, GAO reported its findings from its study of twenty-five foreign militaries, with special focus on Israel, Canada, Germany and Sweden. According to its final report, "Military officials in all four countries said that the presence of homosexuals in the military is not an issue and has not created problems in the functioning of military units." A key factor, said the report, was that homosexuals are reluctant to openly admit their sexual orientation even once the ban is lifted.

Rand researchers concluded that sexual orientation alone was "not germane" in determining who should serve.

---

5. In July 1993, Rand [Corporation] researchers at the National Defense Research Institute, a think tank founded by the Air Force, completed a study commissioned by Defense Secretary Les Aspin. Prepared by over 70 social scientists based on evidence from six countries and data analyses from hundreds of studies of cohesion, [it] concluded that sexual orientation alone was "not germane" in determining who should serve. Rand found that "none of the militaries studied for this report believe their effectiveness as an organization has been impaired or reduced as a result of the inclusion of homosexuals." In Canada, where the ban had just ended, Rand found "no resignations (despite previous threats to quit), no problems with recruitment, and no diminution of cohesion, morale, or organizational effectiveness." The same conclusions were reached about Israel. The study reported that even in those countries where gays were allowed to serve, "in none of these societies is homosexuality widely accepted by a majority of the population."

1. Part of the Rand study examined police and fire departments in several U.S. cities, which it regarded as "the closest possible domestic analog" to the military setting. Rand found that the integration of open gays and lesbians—the status of most departments in the United States—actually enhanced cohesion and improved the police department's community standing and organizational effectiveness. A Palm Center study of the San Diego Police Department in 2001 echoed the finding, adding that nondiscrimination policies in police and fire departments did not impair effectiveness even though many departments were characterized as highly homophobic.

2. The U.S. Army Research Institute for the Behavioral and Social Sciences studied the situation and concluded in a report released in 1994 that anticipated damage to readiness never materialized after the ban was lifted: "Negative consequences predicted in the areas of recruitment, employment, attrition, retention, and cohesion and morale have not occurred since the policy was changed."

3. A 2000 report from the UK Ministry of Defence said the lifting of the ban was "hailed as a solid achievement" that was "introduced smoothly with fewer problems than might have been expected." The changes had "no discernible impact" on recruitment. There was "widespread acceptance of the new policy," and military members generally "demonstrated a mature and pragmatic approach" to the change. There were no reported problems with homosexuals harassing heterosexuals, and there were "no reported difficulties of note concerning homophobic behavior amongst Service Personnel." The report concluded that "there has been a marked lack of reaction" to the change.

4. In 2000, after Britain lifted its ban, the Palm Center at the University of California, Santa Barbara, conducted exhaustive studies to assess the effects of openly gay service in Britain, Israel, Canada, and Australia. Researchers there reviewed over six hundred documents and contacted every identifiable professional with expertise on the policy change, including military officers, government leaders, academic researchers, journalists who covered the issue, veterans, and nongovernmental observers. Palm found that not one person had observed any impact or any effect at all that "undermined military performance, readiness, or cohesion, led to increased difficulties in recruiting or retention, or increased the rate of HIV infection among the troops." Palm researchers found that, "in each case, although many heterosexual soldiers [continued] to object to homosexuality, the military's emphasis on conduct and equal standards was sufficient for encouraging service members to work together as a team" without undermining cohesion.

5. A 2001 paper in the peer-reviewed journal of civil-military relations, *Armed Forces & Society*, argues that Israel's 1993 decision to lift its gay ban did not influence military performance. It then assesses three arguments raised by experts who claim that Israeli experiences are not relevant for determining what would happen if the U.S. Congress and Pentagon lifted the American gay ban. In particular, it assesses the claims that most gay Israeli combat soldiers do not disclose their sexuality to peers, that some receive special treatment, and that cultural differences distinguish the U.S. and Israeli cases. The authors argue that the Israeli experience is not identical to the situation in the U.S., but that its lessons are instructive and lend weight to the claim that American military effectiveness would not decline if known homosexuals were allowed to serve.

6. A 2002 article in *International Security*, "A Modest Proposal: Privacy as a Flawed Rationale for the Exclusion of Gays and Lesbians from the U.S. Military," argues that lifting the gay ban will not undermine heterosexual privacy. Heterosexual service members already shower with known homosexuals, and according to research, lifting the ban is unlikely to substantially increase the number who come out. Additionally, despite the presence of opposition in the ranks, few heterosexual service members are "extremely uncomfortable" around homosexuals, and discomfort that does exist will diminish after lifting the ban. Finally, same-sex desire and same-sex sexual encounters would occur even if all homosexuals were eliminated from the military. The study also concludes that the ban itself enables systematic invasions of heterosexual privacy.

7. A decade after "don't ask, don't tell" was formulated, a study was published in *Parameters*, the official journal of the Army War College, arguing that lifting bans on homosexual personnel does not threaten unit cohesion or undermine military effectiveness. The study was entitled "Don't Ask, Don't Tell: Is the Gay Ban Based on Military Necessity?"

8. In 2005, The U.S. Military Academy at West Point awarded the BG Carroll E. Adams award for best thesis to a paper entitled "Don't Ask, Don't Tell, Don't Be: A Philosophical Analysis of the Gay Ban in the U.S. Military," by the cadet, Alexander Raggio. It was the first time a military service academy granted an award to a paper about gays in the military. The thesis argues that "don't ask, don't tell" is out of step with the values of the military and the nation, and widens the gap between civilian and military culture. It concludes that the "personal prejudices" and "faulty logic" that undergird the

policy "not only fail to meet standards for reasonable policy but undermine the very legitimacy of the institution Army policy should serve."

9. A January 2008 article in *Armed Forces & Society* presents original empirical research to argue that the "don't ask, don't tell" policy harms the military's reputation in several important ways: it is inconsistent with public opinion, it prompts many journalists to criticize the armed forces while attracting almost no favorable media coverage, it provides a vehicle for antimilitary protesters to portray military culture as conflicting with widely accepted civilian values, and it is inconsistent with the views of junior enlisted service members.

10. In July 2008, a bipartisan panel of retired flag officers released a report called the "Report of the General/Flag Officers' Study Group," that represented what John Shalikashvili called "one of the most comprehensive evaluations of the issue of gays in the military since the Rand study" in 1993. The panel, which studied the issue for over a year by drawing on live and written testimony from experts and a review of literature, found that lifting the ban is "unlikely to pose any significant risk to morale, good order, discipline, or cohesion."

A 2000 report from the UK Ministry of Defence said the lifting of the [gay] ban was "hailed as a solid achievement" that was "introduced smoothly with fewer problems than might have been expected."

---

1. In October 2009, *Joint Force Quarterly*, a top military journal published for the Chairman of the Joint Chiefs of Staff, published a study entitled "The Efficacy of 'Don't Ask, Don't Tell'" written by Col. Om Prakash, an

active duty officer in the Air Force. The report found "there is no scientific evidence to support the claim that unit cohesion will be negatively affected if homosexuals serve openly." Based on this research, it concludes that "it is not time for the administration to reexamine the issue; rather it is time for the administration to examine how to implement the repeal of the ban." The article was selected as the first-place winner of the Secretary of Defense National Security Essay competition.

2. A 2009 study by the University of Florida professor Bonnie Moradi and the Rand researcher Laura Miller entitled "Attitudes of Iraq and Afghanistan War Veterans toward Gay and Lesbian Service Members," and published in *Armed Forces & Society*, was the first-ever statistical analysis of whether openly gay service has any impact on military readiness. The study shows that knowing a gay or lesbian unit member has no bearing on the unit's cohesion, concluding that "the data indicated no associations between knowing a lesbian or gay unit member and ratings of perceived unit cohesion or readiness."

3. A 2009 study published in the journal *Military Psychology* has documented the tangible costs of forcing service members to conceal their identities. The study, "Sexual Orientation Disclosure, Concealment, Harassment, and Military Cohesion: Perceptions of LGBT [lesbian, gay, bisexual, and transgender] Military Veterans," is the first empirical analysis of the relationship between sexual orientation concealment and unit cohesion in the military. The study found that sexual orientation disclosure is positively related to unit cohesion, while concealment and harassment are related negatively, meaning they appear to reduce cohesion. This means that the only empirical evidence linking assessing the relationship be-

tween open homosexuality and unit cohesion shows the link to be positive, not negative, because of the damage of the closet to the morale and readiness of gay troops, and by extension to the readiness of units.

4. Lt. Col. Irene V. Glaeser wrote a study entitled "Don't Ask, Don't Tell: Time for Change," at the U.S. Army War College as a 2009 Strategy Research Project as part of a paper submitted for a Master of Strategic Studies Degree. The paper cites "exhaustive studies" of both "don't ask, don't tell" and the experience of foreign militaries to argue that openly gay service does not impair the military and that current policy "needs to be revised and lifted." Glaeser states that the U.S. has "entered an era of persistent conflict," and must be "broad-minded and agile enough to adapt."

5. In Spring 2010, Air University Press, the government-owned publishing arm of the U.S. Air Force, will publish a comprehensive volume on diversity in the Armed Forces. The book, entitled *Attitudes Aren't Free: Thinking Deeply about Diversity in the US Armed Forces*, offers a range of perspectives and a framework for improving policy on religious expression, open homosexuality, race, gender, and ethics in the Armed Forces. Palm researchers have written a chapter for the book in light of President [Barack] Obama's stated intention to end "don't ask, don't tell." The chapter addresses questions about how best to execute and manage the transition from exclusion of openly gay personnel to inclusion. The Palm chapter addresses the political, legal, regulatory, and organizational steps necessary to ensure that the implementation process goes smoothly.

The Pentagon Concludes That Repealing DADT Poses a Low Risk to Military Effectiveness

Carter F. Ham and Jeh Charles Johnson

Carter F. Ham is a general in the US Army, and Jeh Charles Johnson is general counsel for the US Department of Defense. They cochaired the working group tasked by the secretary of defense with assessing the impacts of a repeal of "Don't Ask Don't Tell."

On March 2, 2010, the Secretary of Defense appointed the two of us to co-chair a working group to undertake a comprehensive review of the impacts of repeal, should it occur, of Section 654 of Title 10 of the United States Code, commonly known as the "Don't Ask, Don't Tell" law. In this effort, we were aided by a highly dedicated team of 49 military and 19 civilian personnel from across the Department of Defense and the Military Services. Our assignment from the Secretary was two-fold: 1) assess the impact of repeal of Don't Ask, Don't Tell on military readiness, military effectiveness, unit cohesion, recruiting, retention, and family readiness; and 2) recommend appropriate changes, if necessary, to existing regulations, policies, and guidance in the event of repeal. The Secretary directed us to deliver our assessment and recommendations to him by December 1, 2010. This document constitutes our report of that assessment and our recommendations. The Secretary also directed us to develop a plan of action to support implementation of a repeal of Don't Ask, Don't Tell. That plan accompanies this report.

At the outset, it is important to note the environment in which we conducted our work: the Nation's military has been at war on several fronts for over 9 years. Much is being demanded from the force. The men and women in uniform who risk their lives to defend our Nation are, along with their families, stretched and stressed, and have faced years of multiple and lengthy deployments to Iraq, Afghanistan, and elsewhere. Some question the wisdom of taking on the emotional and difficult issue of Don't Ask, Don't Tell on top of all else. For these and other reasons, the Secretary directed that we "thoroughly, objectively and methodically examine all aspects of this question," and include, most importantly, the views of our men and women in uniform. . . .

We are convinced that the U.S. military can adjust [to] and accommodate this change, just as it has others in history.

To our knowledge, our nine-month review and engagement of the Force was the largest and most comprehensive in the history of the U.S. military, on any personnel-related matter.

Based on all we saw and heard, our assessment is that, when coupled with the prompt implementation of the recommendations we offer below, the risk of repeal of Don't Ask, Don't Tell to overall military effectiveness is low. We conclude that, while a repeal of Don't Ask, Don't Tell will likely, in the short term, bring about some limited and isolated disruption to unit cohesion and retention, we do not believe this disruption will be widespread or long-lasting, and can be adequately addressed by the recommendations we offer below. Longer term, with a continued and sustained commitment to core values of leadership, professionalism, and respect for all, we are convinced that the U.S. military can adjust [to] and accommodate this change, just as it has others in history. . . .

Support from Service Members

The results of the Service member survey reveal a widespread attitude among a solid majority of Service members that repeal of Don't Ask, Don't Tell will not have a negative impact on their ability to conduct their military mission. The survey was conducted by Westat, a research firm with a long track record of conducting surveys for the U.S. military. The survey was one of the largest in the history of the military. We heard from over 115,000 Service members, or 28% of those solicited. Given the large number of respondents, the margin of error for the results was less than ±1%, and the response rate was average for the U.S. military.

The results of the survey are best represented by the answers to three questions:

- When asked about how having a Service member in their immediate unit who said he or she is gay would affect the unit's ability to "work together to get the job done," 70% of Service members predicted it would have a positive, mixed, or no effect.

- When asked "in your career, have you ever worked in a unit with a co-worker that you believed to be homosexual," 69% of Service members reported that they had.

- When asked about the actual experience of serving in a unit with a co-worker who they believed was gay or lesbian, 92% stated that the unit's "ability to work together" was "very good," "good," or "neither good nor poor."

Consistently, the survey results revealed a large group of around 50–55% of Service members who thought that repeal of Don't Ask, Don't Tell would have mixed or no effect; another 15–20% who said repeal would have a positive effect; and about 30% who said it would have a negative effect. The results of the spouse survey are consistent. When spouses were asked about whether repeal of Don't Ask, Don't Tell would affect their preference for their Service member's future plans to stay in the military, 74% said repeal would have no effect, while only 12% said "I would want my spouse to leave earlier."

The reality is that there are gay men and lesbians already serving in today's U.S. military, and most Service members recognize this.

To be sure, these survey results reveal a significant minority—around 30% overall (and 40–60% in the Marine Corps and in various combat arms specialties)—who predicted in some form and to some degree negative views or concerns about the impact of a repeal of Don't Ask, Don't Tell. Any personnel policy change for which a group that size predicts negative consequences must be approached with caution. However, there are a number of other factors that still lead us to conclude that the risk of repeal to overall military effectiveness is low.

The reality is that there are gay men and lesbians already serving in today's U.S. military, and most Service members recognize this. As stated before, 69% of the force recognizes that they have at some point served in a unit with a co-worker they believed to be gay or lesbian. Of those who have actually had this experience in their career, 92% stated that the unit's "ability to work together" was "very good," "good," or "neither good nor poor," while only 8% stated it was "poor" or "very poor." Anecdotally, we also heard a number of Service members tell us about a leader, co-worker, or fellow Service member they greatly liked, trusted, or admired, who they later learned was gay; and how once that person's sexual orientation was revealed to them, it made little or no difference to the relationship. Both the survey results and our own engagement of the force convinced us that when Service members had the actual experience of serving with someone they believe to be gay, in general, unit performance was not affected negatively by this added dimension.

Aside from the moral and religious objections to homosexuality, much of the concern about "open" service is driven by misperceptions and stereotypes.

Concerns About Open Service

Yet, a frequent response among Service members at information exchange forums, when asked about the widespread recognition that gay men and lesbians are already in the military, were words to the effect of: "yes, but I don't *know* they are gay." Put another way, the concern with repeal among many is with "open" service.

In the course of our assessment, it became apparent to us that, aside from the moral and religious objections to homosexuality, much of the concern about "open" service is driven by misperceptions and stereotypes about what it would mean if gay Service members were allowed to be "open" about their sexual orientation. Repeatedly, we heard Service members express the view that "open" homosexuality would lead to widespread and overt displays of effeminacy among men, homosexual promiscuity, harassment and unwelcome advances within units, invasions of personal privacy, and an overall erosion of standards of conduct, unit cohesion, and morality. Based on our review, however, we conclude that these concerns about gay and lesbian Service members who are permitted to be "open" about their sexual orientation are exaggerated, and not consistent with the reported experiences of many Service members.

In today's civilian society, where there is no law that requires gay men and lesbians to conceal their sexual orientation in order to keep their job, most gay men and lesbians still tend to be discreet about their personal lives, and guarded about the people with whom they share information about their sexual orientation. We believe that, in the military environment, this would be true even more so. According to a survey conducted by [the] RAND [Corporation] of a limited number of individuals who anonymously self-identified as gay and lesbian Service members, even if Don't Ask, Don't Tell were repealed, only 15% of gay and lesbian Service members would like to have their sexual orientation known to everyone in their unit. This conclusion is also consistent with what we heard from gay Service members in the course of this review:

> "Personally, I don't feel that this is something I should have to 'disclose.' Straight people don't have to disclose their orientation. I will just be me. I will bring my family to family events. I will put family pictures on my desk. I am not going to go up to people and say, hi there—I'm gay."

> "I think a lot of people think there is going to be this big 'outing' and people flaunting their gayness, but they forget that we're in the military. That stuff isn't supposed to be done during duty hours regardless if you're gay or straight."

If gay and lesbian Service members in today's U.S. military were permitted to make reference to their sexual orientation, while subject to the same standards of conduct as all other Service members, we assess that most would continue to be private and discreet about their personal lives. This discretion would occur for reasons having nothing to do with law, but everything to do with a desire to fit in, co-exist, and succeed in the military environment.

As one gay Service member stated:

> "I don't think it's going to be such a big, huge, horrible thing that DoD [Department of Defense] is telling everyone its going to be. If it is repealed, everyone will look around their spaces to see if anyone speaks up. They'll hear crickets

for a while. A few flamboyant guys and tough girls will join to rock the boat and make a scene. Their actions and bad choices will probably get them kicked out. After a little time has gone by, then a few of us will speak up. And instead of a deluge of panic and violence . . . there'll be a ripple on the water's surface that dissipates quicker than you can watch."

In communications with gay and lesbian current and former Service members, we repeatedly heard a patriotic desire to serve and defend the Nation, subject to the same rules as everyone else. In the words of one gay Service member, repeal would simply "take a knife out of my back. . . . You have no idea what it is like to have to serve in silence." Most said they did not desire special treatment, to use the military for social experimentation, or to advance a social agenda. Some of those separated under Don't Ask, Don't Tell would welcome the opportunity to rejoin the military if permitted. From them, we heard expressed many of the same values that we heard over and over again from Service members at large— love of country, honor, respect, integrity, and service over self. We simply cannot square the reality of these people with the perceptions about "open" service.

The percentage of those who predict negative effects are higher in combat arms units.

Given that we are in a time of war, the combat arms communities across all Services required special focus and analysis. Though the survey results demonstrate a solid majority of the overall U.S. military who predict mixed, positive or no effect in the event of repeal, these percentages are lower, and the percentage of those who predict negative effects are higher, in combat arms units. For example, . . . while the percentage of the overall U.S. military that predicts negative or very negative effects on their unit's ability to "work together to get the job done" is 30%, the percentage is 43% for the Marine Corps, 48% within Army combat arms units, and 58% within Marine combat arms units.

Risks of Repeal in Warfighting Units

However, while a higher percentage of Service members in warfighting units *predict* negative effects of repeal, the percentage distinctions between warfighting units and the entire military are almost non-existent when asked about the *actual* experience of serving in a unit with someone believed to be gay. For example, when those in the overall military were asked about the experience of working with someone they believed to be gay or lesbian, 92% stated that their unit's "ability to work together," was "very good," "good" or "neither good nor poor." Meanwhile, in response to the same question, the percentage is 89% for those in Army combat arms units and 84% for those in Marine combat arms units—all very high percentages. Anecdotally, we heard much the same. As one special operations force warfighter told us, "We have a gay guy [in the unit]. He's big, he's mean, and he kills lots of bad guys. No one cared that he was gay."

Thus, the survey results reflecting actual experience, our other engagements, and the lessons of history lead us to conclude that the risks of repeal within warfighting units, while higher than the force generally, remain within acceptable levels when coupled with our recommendations for implementation.

The survey results also reveal, within warfighting units, negative predictions about serving alongside gays decrease when in "intense combat situations." . . . For example, 67% of those in Marine combat arms units predict working alongside a gay man or lesbian will have a negative effect on their unit's effectiveness in completing its mission "in a field environment or out at sea." By contrast, in response to the same question, but during "an intense combat situation," the percentage drops to 48%. . . . While 48% indicates a significant level of concern, the near 20-point difference in these two environments reflects that, in a combat situation, the warfighter appreciates that differences with those within his unit become less important than defeating the common enemy.

Our assessment also took account of the fact that the Nation is at war on several fronts, and, for a period of over nine years, the U.S. military has been fully engaged, and has faced the stress and demands of frequent and lengthy deployments. We conclude that repeal can be implemented now, provided it is done in manner that minimizes the burden on leaders in deployed areas. Our recommended implementation plan does just that. . . . The primary concern is for the added requirement that will be created by the training and education associated with repeal. We are cognizant of this concern, but note that during this time of war, the Services have undertaken education and training in deployed areas on a number of important personnel matters. These education and training initiatives have included increased emphasis on sexual assault prevention and response, suicide prevention, and training to detect indications of behavioral health problems. The conduct of these programs in deployed areas indicates that training and education associated with a repeal of Don't Ask, Don't Tell can be accommodated. We assess this to be the case, in large part because our recommendations in this report involve a minimalist approach to changes in policies, and education and training to reiterate existing policies in a sexual orientation-neutral manner.

The risks of repeal within warfighting units, while higher than the force generally, remain within acceptable levels.

It is also the case that the results of the survey indicate that, in this war-time environment, a solid majority of Service members believe that repeal will have positive, mixed, or no effect. Most of those surveyed joined our military after September 11, 2001, and have known nothing but a military at war.

Lessons of History

Our assessment here is also informed by the lessons of history in this country. Though there are fundamental differences between matters of race, gender, and sexual orientation, we believe the U.S. military's prior experiences with racial and gender integration are relevant. In the late 1940s and early 1950s, our military took on the racial integration of its ranks, *before* the country at large had done so. Our military then was many times larger than it is today, had just returned from World War II, and was in the midst of Cold War tensions and the Korean War. By our assessment, the resistance to change at that time was far more intense: surveys of the military revealed opposition to racial integration of the Services at levels as high as 80–90%. Some of our best-known and most-revered military leaders from the World War II era voiced opposition to the integration of blacks into the military, making strikingly similar predictions of the negative impact on unit cohesion. But by 1953, 95% of all African-American soldiers were serving in racially integrated units, while public buses in Montgomery, Alabama and other cities were still racially segregated. Today, the U.S. military is probably the most racially diverse and integrated institution in the country—one in which an African American rose through the ranks to become the senior-most military officer in the country 20 years before Barack Obama was elected President.

The story is similar when it came to the integration of women into the military. In 1948, women were limited to 2% of active duty personnel in each Service, with significant limitations on the roles they could perform. Currently, women make up 14% of the force, and are permitted to serve in 92% of the occupational specialties. Along the way to gender integration, many of our Nation's military leaders predicted dire consequences for unit cohesion and military effectiveness if women were allowed to serve in large numbers. As with racial integration, this experience has not always been smooth. But, the consensus is the same: the introduction and integration of women into the force has made our military stronger.

The general lesson we take from these transformational experiences in history is that in matters of personnel change within the military, predictions and surveys tend to overestimate negative consequences, and underestimate the U.S. military's ability to adapt and incorporate within its ranks the diversity that is reflective of American society at large.

Our conclusions are also informed by the experiences of our foreign allies. To be sure, there is no perfect comparator to the U.S. military, and the cultures and attitudes toward homosexuality vary greatly among nations of the world. However, in recent times a number of other countries have transitioned to policies that permit open military service by gay men and lesbians. These include the United Kingdom, Canada, Australia, Germany, Italy, and Israel. Significantly, prior to change, surveys of the militaries in Canada and the U.K. indicated much higher levels of resistance than our own survey results—as high as 65% for some areas—but the actual implementation of change in those countries went much more smoothly than expected, with little or no disruption. . . .

In sum, we are convinced the U.S. military can make this change, even during this time of war.

Foreign Militaries Report No Harm to Unit Cohesion or Morale When Gays Serve Openly

Steve Chapman

Steve Chapman is a syndicated columnist and an editorial writer for the Chicago Tribune.

There are lots of reasons for excluding gays and lesbians from the military. But current supporters of the "don't ask, don't tell" policy insist that, really, it all comes down to cohesion. Keep gays out, and soldiers will stick together through thick and thin. Let gays in, and every platoon will disintegrate like a sand castle in the surf.

[Senator] John McCain sounded this theme at a Senate hearing the other day [in February 2010], arguing that the existing law rests on the belief "that the essence of military capability is good order and unit cohesion, and that any practice which puts those goals at unacceptable risk can be restricted." A group of retired military officers said the ban on gays serves "to protect unit cohesion and morale."

Maybe this concern is what really underlies the exclusion of gays and lesbians. But I'm not so sure. In 2007, Gen. Peter Pace, then chairman of the Joint Chiefs of Staff, was asked about it, and he offered a different rationale. "I believe homosexual acts between two individuals are immoral and that we should not condone immoral acts," he said. Could the opposition stem mostly from a simple aversion to gays and their ways?

It's not completely implausible that in a military environment, open homosexuality might wreak havoc on order and morale. But the striking thing about these claims is that they exist in a fact-free zone. From all the dire predictions, you would think a lifting of the ban would be an unprecedented leap into the dark, orchestrated by people who know nothing of the demands of military life.

As it happens, we now have a wealth of experience on which to evaluate the policy. When you examine it, you discover the reason McCain and Co. make a point of never mentioning it.

Experiences of Other Nations

A couple of dozen countries already allow gays in uniform—including allies that have fought alongside our troops, such as Britain, Canada, and Australia. Just as there is plenty of opposition in the U.S. ranks, there was plenty of opposition when they changed their policies.

In Canada, 45 percent of service members said they would not work with gay colleagues, and a majority of British soldiers and sailors rejected the idea. There were warnings that hordes of military personnel would quit and promising youngsters would refuse to enlist.

A couple of dozen countries already allow gays in uniform—including allies that have fought alongside our troops, such as Britain, Canada, and Australia.

But when the new day arrived, it turned out to be a big, fat non-event. The Canadian government reported "no effect." The British government observed "a marked lack of reaction." An Australian veterans group that opposed admitting gays later admitted that the services "have not had a lot of difficulty in this area."

Israel, being small, surrounded by hostile powers, and obsessed with security, can't afford to jeopardize its military strength for the sake of prissy ventures in political correctness. But its military not only accepts gays, it provides benefits to their same-sex partners, as it does with spouses. Has that policy sapped Israel's military might? Its enemies don't seem eager to test the proposition.

U.S. Experience with Gay Soldiers

You could argue that none of these experiences is relevant, since, being Americans, we are utterly unique. But our soldiers don't seem to have any trouble fighting alongside gay soldiers from allied nations.

All recent experience argues that the American military would adapt fine to accepting gays.

Not only that, but it turns out the U.S. military itself has tried the same policy with satisfactory results. Former Joint Chiefs Chairman Gen. John Shalikashvili has pointed out that "enforcement of the ban was suspended without problems during the Persian Gulf War, and there were no reports of angry departures."

That's right: We fought a war without the ban, and we won. In a pinch, our heterosexual men and women in uniform confirmed, they can function perfectly well amid openly gay colleagues.

That shouldn't be surprising, since the military requires its members to live with all sorts of people in close quarters and demanding conditions. A lot of recruits would be more leery of bunking next to an ex-con than a homosexual, but the military admits hundreds of felons each year, including some violent ones. If unit cohesion can survive the presence of killers, rapists, and child molesters, why would it shatter on contact with gays and lesbians?

All recent experience argues that the American military would adapt fine to accepting gays. But when it comes to actual real-world evidence, supporters of the ban don't ask, and they don't tell.

Gays Are Already Serving Honorably in the US Military Without Causing Harm

Alan M. Steinman

Alan M. Steinman is a retired rear admiral with the United States Public Health Service and the US Coast Guard, as well as the former surgeon general of the Coast Guard.

Gay, lesbian, and bisexual (GLB) Americans are serving their country honorably in every branch of our Armed Forces in this time of war. Yet the "Don't Ask, Don't Tell" (DADT) law requires them to serve in silence, to lie about who they are, and to violate the very code of honor they are defending by their service. Gay servicemen and women are fighting for their country, being wounded for their country, and even dying for their country. Yet Congress and the Pentagon seem unaware that these brave men and women have to serve in fear of being discovered, fear of being kicked out simply for who they are, or worse, fear of harassment or violence. Our nation needs to appreciate that gay men and women in the military are as patriotic, physically and mentally fit, and mission capable as their straight counterparts. In the Armed Forces, courage, commitment and devotion to duty matter, not sexual orientation.

Since I came out publicly in 2003 on the 10th anniversary of DADT, I have had the privilege of meeting hundreds of GLBT [gay, lesbian, bisexual, and transgender] veterans, many of them still on active duty. Surprisingly, many of them are also serving with the knowledge of their peers, and sometimes even with the knowledge of their commands, all without problems. Their experiences, and those of the estimated 65,000

GLB service men and women currently on active duty will help convince the American public, Congress, and the Administration that DADT is unnecessary and harmful to our national security.

At a time when our nation struggles to recruit capable service members, it cannot continue to exclude gay men and women who are willing and able to serve.

The Impact of DADT

The "Don't Ask, Don't Tell" law dates from 1992, when then Presidential candidate Bill Clinton promised to allow GLB Americans to serve openly in the military. On January 29, 1993, shortly after his inauguration, President Clinton suspended the existing Department of Defense policy which banned gay and lesbian personnel from military service. However, the Joint Chiefs of Staff and influential members of Congress vehemently opposed the President's attempt to permanently lift the ban. This led to six months of intense Congressional and Administration discussions and hearings on the issue. The end result was the infamous "Don't Ask, Don't Tell" law. It was inserted into the 1994 National Defense Authorization Act and represented a so-called compromise between the President, who wanted to allow GLB members to serve openly, and the Pentagon and its Congressional allies who wanted to totally ban them. Under DADT, the military would not inquire about the sexual orientation of current and future service members. GLB men and women would be allowed to serve in the U.S. Armed Forces unless they declared they are gay, attempted to marry a person of the same sex, or engaged in homosexual conduct. Service members who were discovered to be homosexual would be subject to dismissal. The compromise did nothing to protect GLB service members from harassment, and it paradoxically resulted in a dramatic increase in GLB discharges.

Over the next 13 years, nearly 11,000 GLB members were kicked out of the military as a result of DADT, at a cost of nearly $400 million. Thousands more GLB service members have voluntarily left the military because they could no longer tolerate living a lie in order to serve. At a time when our nation struggles to recruit capable service members, it cannot continue to exclude the tens of thousands of gay men and women who are willing and able to serve. More than an issue of civil rights, it is an issue of national security.

Supporters of the DADT policy argue that unit cohesion and morale would be damaged if openly gay and lesbian people were allowed to serve. Dozens of studies and the experiences of many key American allies have shown that these arguments are without merit. Furthermore, this policy presumes that junior enlisted service members, mostly young men, would be uncomfortable serving next to gays. Yet national polls in 2004 and 2005 show that a large majority of Americans support gays and lesbians serving openly. More significantly, a recent poll of junior enlisted service members, the segment of the armed forces presumed least willing to work alongside openly GLB members, shows a majority in favor of GLB members serving openly. Finally, the experiences of the many GLB members who are currently serving without problems, many of the them in combat, despite being known to be gay, lesbian or bisexual, demonstrates that the entire underlying premise of DADT is false. Now, more than ever, Congress needs to repeal DADT.

CHAPTER 3

Do Members of the Military Support Ending "Don't Ask Don't Tell"?

Overview: What Service Members Think About Ending "Don't Ask Don't Tell"

The Week

The Week is an online magazine offering commentary and analysis of the day's breaking news and current events and arts and entertainment.

Editor's Note: On December 18, 2010, Congress passed the Don't Ask Don't Tell Repeal Act of 2010, authorizing the president, the secretary of defense, and the chairman of the Joint Chiefs of Staff to certify that repeal "is consistent with the standards of military readiness, military effectiveness, unit cohesion, and re-cruiting and retention of the Armed Forces." After certification, there was then a sixty-day waiting period before "Don't Ask Don't Tell" was formally repealed.

The Pentagon this week [November 30, 2010,] released a long-awaited report on the potential repeal of "Don't ask, don't tell," [DADT] saying the[re] is little risk to letting gay and lesbians serve openly in the military. Seven out of 10 members of the armed forces said the impact of lifting the ban would be "positive, mixed, or of no consequence at all." The report energized people on both sides of the issue as the lame-duck Senate prepares for a possible vote on repealing the law before Christmas. Aside from soldiers, where do other in-fluential players line up in this contentious debate?

Those Who Are Pro-Repeal

The public. A majority of Americans favor repealing DADT, according to a new poll. Fifty-eight percent of respondents to the Pew survey said gays should be allowed to openly serve in the military, with just 27 percent saying they were opposed to it. "These opinions have changed little in recent years," noted the pollsters. "Since 2005 . . . roughly 60 percent have consistently favored" allowing gays in the military.

Although a majority of soldiers as a whole are either in favor of, or ambivalent about serving alongside gay soldiers, the Marine Corps is overwhelmingly against it.

The chairman of the Joint Chiefs of Staff. Admiral Mike Mullen, the highest-ranking officer in the United States Armed Forces, told a Senate committee he was in favor of repeal in February [2010]. He said it was "the right thing to do," and added that he was personally against effectively ordering soldiers to "lie about who they are in order to defend their fellow citizens." Mullen made it clear he was stating his own opinion, not that of the military as a whole.

The president. On the campaign trail in 2008, Barack Obama vowed that he would repeal DADT, but he decided once he became president that he wanted the military's support before making good on his promise. Now that the Pentagon survey is complete, Obama has reiterated his desire to scrap a law that, he says, "weakens our national security, diminishes our military readiness and violates fundamental principles of American fairness and equality."

The courts. In September [2010], a federal judge ruled that DADT was unconstitutional. Discharging openly gay soldiers from the military is in violation of the First and Fifth Amendments, ruled U.S. District Judge Virginia Phillips. But the Obama administration appealed the ruling, on the basis that it was up to Congress, not the courts, to change the policy.

Those Who Are Against Repeal

The Marine Corps. Although a majority of soldiers as a whole are either in favor of, or ambivalent about serving alongside gay soldiers, the Marine Corps is overwhelming against it. The Pentagon survey found that two-thirds (67 percent) of Marines in combat roles said repealing DADT would harm their units' "cohesiveness."

The military top brass. Before the Pentagon survey was completed, the heads of the Army, Marines, Air Force, and Navy expressed their opposition to a premature repeal of DADT. All agreed it was essential to consider the views of the soldiers themselves before the Senate voted on repeal. All four are scheduled to testify on the Pentagon survey before the Senate Armed Services Committee on Friday [December 3, 2010].

Sen. John McCain. The Arizona senator's view on DADT shifted during the course of this year. Previously, the war hero and former Republican presidential candidate has said he would support repeal if the military agreed it was a good idea. But following Admiral Mullen's statement in February, McCain told reporters he was "disappointed" at the joint chiefs chairman's testimony. "At this moment of immense hardship for our armed services, we should not be seeking to overturn the 'don't ask, don't tell' policy," he said. He has not yet responded to the Pentagon survey.

Most Troops Are Amenable to Repealing "Don't Ask Don't Tell"

Michael Sheridan and Richard Sisk

Michael Sheridan and Richard Sisk are staff writers for the Daily News, a New York City daily newspaper.

The civilian and military leaders of the nation's armed forces urged Congress Tuesday [November 30, 2010,] to repeal the Don't Ask, Don't Tell [DADT] policy based on a survey showing that most troops are okay with gays serving openly.

Defense Secretary Robert Gates said it was a simple matter of right and wrong. "A policy that requires people to lie about themselves to me seems fundamentally flawed," Gates said.

Adm. Mike Mullen, chairman of the Joint Chiefs of Staff, said getting rid of DADT would not have a major impact on morale or readiness as many feared: "This is a policy that we can do and we can do it in a relatively low-risk fashion."

Troop Survey

Mullen and Gates spoke at a Pentagon briefing on a massive survey of active duty troops that showed 70% believe a repeal of DADT would have either a positive effect or no effect on their ability to complete missions.

The study is based upon answers provided by nearly 115,000 troops, along with 44,200 military spouses. The study group also visited various military bases and held town hall-style meetings with service members.

Those results appear to echo those found in a Pew Research Center survey last month [October 2010], which indicated 58% of Americans favored allowing gays to serve openly in the military.

There were higher levels of "discomfort" about serving alongside gays among combat troops in the infantry and artillery.

Gates pressed the Senate to enact repeal quickly in the lameduck session, saying that avoiding the issue would amount to "rolling the dice" on the courts taking action.

Gates conceded there were higher levels of "discomfort" about serving alongside gays among combat troops in the infantry and artillery.

"Those findings remain a source of concern to the service chiefs and to me," Gates said.

Opposition to gays serving was highest in the Marine Corps, where nearly half the marines are opposed. The Navy was the most welcoming, according to the Pentagon review.

Lt. Col. Victor Fehrenbach, a decorated Air Force fighter pilot currently fighting discharge under the "Don't Ask, Don't Tell" policy, said the survey was proof that homosexuality "is a nonissue in the military."

"I live it every day" as an openly gay officer, Fehrenbach said.

The survey said the current rules on conduct and fraternization under the Uniform Code of Military Justice would apply if "Don't Ask, Don't Tell" is repealed.

No separate showers, bathing or living quarters should be provided for gays, the survey noted.

The Defense Secretary and Joint Chiefs Chairman Support Repeal of "Don't Ask Don't Tell"

Kerry Eleveld

Kerry Eleveld is a journalist and political editor for The Advocate, *a national gay and lesbian newsmagazine.*

Defense secretary Robert Gates, chairman of the Joint Chiefs Adm. Mike Mullen, and the cochairs of the Pentagon's working group study delivered a uniformed opinion at a Senate hearing Thursday [December 2, 2010,] that "don't ask, don't tell" [DADT] should be repealed before the end of the year.

Admiral Mullen told members of the Senate Armed Services Committee that his personal opinion that repeal was "the right thing to do" was now his professional opinion after reviewing the Pentagon's comprehensive study.

"Back in February, when I testified to this sentiment, I also said that I believed the men and women of the Armed Forces could accommodate such a change. But I did not know it for a fact," Mullen said. "Now I do."

Secretary Gates added what has become a familiar refrain from him: "I believe this has become a matter of some urgency because, as we have seen this past year, the judicial branch is becoming involved in this issue and it is only a matter of a time before the federal courts are drawn once more into the fray."

Later in the hearing Gates added that a court-imposed end to the policy would give the military "zero time to prepare" and called that scenario "a very high risk to the force."

Gen. Carter Ham, a cochair of the study group, followed Gates's lead when he was asked whether he personally believed the law should be repealed by Sen. John McCain, the ranking minority member on the committee and a key detractor of repeal.

General Ham, who has expressed reservations in the past about ending the policy, said that he was personally "very concerned about the timing of the courts."

In light of that, Ham told McCain, "Yes sir, I think it is time to change."

[Defense secretary Robert] Gates added that a court-imposed end to the policy would give the military "zero time to prepare."

Committee chair Sen. Carl Levin asked Ham, who currently commands the Army's forces in Europe, whether he believed he could implement repeal if the Senate were to overturn the policy.

"Mr. Chairman, I'm confident that I can," Ham responded.

Jeh Johnson, general counsel at the Department of Defense and a cochair of the study, underscored fears of sudden judicial action with his professional opinion as an observer of the courts.

"There is a trend that is taking place since the *Lawrence* [v. *Texas*] decision that we need to be mindful of," Johnson said of the fact that judges have grown increasingly likely to side with gays and lesbians since the Supreme Court overturned sodomy laws nationwide in 2003.

Republican Concerns Rebutted

Republican [GOP] senators fixated repeatedly on the fact that the study never specifically asked whether service members believed the policy should be changed.

But Gates called taking a referendum on a policy change "a very dangerous path."

"I can't think of a single precedent in American history of doing a referendum of the forces on a policy issue," he said, responding to a question from GOP senator Roger Wicker. "That's not the way our military has ever worked."

GOP senator Susan Collins, who voted for repeal in committee last spring but joined a Republican filibuster of the larger defense authorization bill in September, noted that the military does not make a habit of polling the forces for their opinions.

"I would point out that our troops are not asked whether they should be deployed to Afghanistan, they're not asked whether we should have a war in Iraq, they're generally not asked," Collins said.

GOP senators also pounded on the fact that of the 400,000 troops solicited for their views on the policy change, only 28% responded to the survey the working group conducted.

But Mullen rebuffed the assertion, saying "it was an extraordinarily positive response" and "more than statistically significant in all the key categories."

Democratic senator Jim Webb agreed with Mullen. Webb explained that he had originally voted against attaching the repeal measure in committee because he "felt very strongly that it was important to listen to the people who are serving, to consider their views."

[Joint Chiefs chairman Mike] Mullen was a uniquely steady, firm, and forceful voice on the necessity of changing the law.

"This is really, in my view, an incredible piece of work," Webb said of the 343-page study. "This report is probably the most crucial piece of information that we have in terms of really objectively moving forward as to how to address the law."

Overall, Mullen was a uniquely steady, firm, and forceful voice on the necessity of changing the law.

"I find the argument that war is not the time to change to be antithetical with our own experience since 2001," Mullen said in his opening statement. "War does not stifle change, it demands it. It does not make change harder, it facilitates it."

At the close of his statement, he said, "For more than 40 years, I have made decisions that affected and even risked the lives of young men and women. You do not have to agree with me on this issue. But don't think for one moment that I haven't carefully considered the impact of the advice I give on those who will have to live with the decisions that advice informs. I would not recommend repeal of this law if I did not believe in my soul it was the right thing to do."

Repeal advocates were overwhelmingly positive about the developments of the day.

Aubrey Sarvis, executive director of the Servicemembers Legal Defense Network, said he was most impressed by "the unity of the senior military leadership in their recommendation to act in the lameduck."

"Senator McCain, as much as he tried, was unable to have any break of ranks among Gates, Mullen, Ham, and Johnson," he said.

But Friday [December 3, 2010,] morning may have a very different tone when the service chiefs of the military branches will fill the same hearing room with their opinions. The chiefs have all expressed their opposition to repeal over the course of hearings in the spring and summer.

"The service chiefs will likely express less enthusiasm for a change in this policy as well as some creative interpretation and cherry-picking of the report data," said Alex Nicholson, executive director of the Servicemembers United. "But at the end of the day, I would expect them all to strongly agree that their respective branches are more than capable of handling and effectively managing the implementation of this policy change."

Veterans and Military Families Support Ending "Don't Ask Don't Tell"

Todd Stenhouse

Todd Stenhouse is a spokesperson for the Courage Campaign, an online organizing network that works for progressive policy changes.

As Congress awaits formal release of the much anticipated Pentagon Study about the military's "Don't Ask Don't Tell [DADT] Policy," thousands of veterans and military families are speaking up for repeal.

More than 10,000 veterans and military families have already signed the petition organized by Iraq War veteran and Congressman Patrick Murphy, the national progressive advocacy group Courage Campaign, and VoteVets.org—a leading political advocacy group for veterans of the wars in Iraq and Afghanistan.

"The politicians who voted against repealing DADT and funding our military in October [2010] have said they want to hear from our troops," said Courage Campaign Chairman and Founder Rick Jacobs. "We're going to make sure they do. Veterans and military families know that supporting our troops during a time of war starts with repealing failed policies that undermine the trust on which combat units depend, deprive those same units of mission critical specialists, and contradict the values that generations of Americans have fought and died to defend."

Broad Support for Repeal

To date, "Don't Ask Don't Tell" has led to the discharge of nearly 14,000 soldiers, sailors, marines and airmen, at a cost to U.S. taxpayers of more than $500 million. This includes hundreds of "mission critical" specialists for which the military has faced shortages in recent years—including pilots, combat engineers, and Arab[ic] linguists. More than 66,000 LGBT [lesbian, gay, bisexual, and transgender] Americans are reported to be serving in the military today, or 2.2% of the total force. As of 2007, twenty two countries that allow open service have deployed troops to serve alongside American forces in Iraq and Afghanistan.

Both inside and outside the military, repeal of "Don't Ask Don't Tell" enjoys broad, bi-partisan support.

"This is an issue I've personally dealt with. In the Marines, one of my proudest moments was being one of the first to successfully defend a gay Marine from being discharged from the service. I've seen—first-hand—how keeping this policy in place hurts the military," said Ashwin Madia, Iraq War Veteran and Interim Chairman of VoteVets.org. "When you strip all the rhetoric away on this issue, it comes down to this: We need to repeal Don't Ask Don't Tell to make our military stronger."

Both inside and outside the military, repeal of "Don't Ask Don't Tell" enjoys broad, bi-partisan support. President [Barack] Obama, a majority of the House and Senate, Secretary of Defense Robert Gates, and Chairman of the Joint Chiefs Mike Mullen, and more than 78% of Americans also support repeal. Media reports have also indicated that the soon to be released Pentagon study will show 70% of the military and military families do not object to repeal.

Among those who have signed the Murphy/Courage Campaign/Vote Vets petition are hundreds of veterans of the wars in Iraq and Afghanistan, thousands more who served in WWII, Korea, Vietnam, the Cold War, Grenada, Panama, the first Gulf War and Bosnia, and thousands of military family members.

"With the recent Defense Department report confirming what we've been saying for years, it's time for both parties to do the right thing and repeal this discriminatory policy that harms national security and wastes taxpayer dollars," Congressman Patrick Murphy said. "The thousands of veterans and military families who have signed these petitions know what it means to support our troops, and I hope Senate Republicans will join them in supporting repeal."

All told, the Courage Campaign and VoteVets have accumulated more than 600,000 signatures for repeal of "Don't Ask Don't Tell." Congressman Murphy, a former West Point professor who successfully led the effort to pass repeal in the House, has pledged to deliver those signatures to Senate Leadership prior to release of the Pentagon study on December 1 [2010].

A Majority of Service Members Are Against a Gay Agenda in the Military

Elaine Donnelly

Elaine Donnelly is president of the Center for Military Readiness, a nonprofit organization that focuses on military personnel issues; she is also a contributing editor for Human Events, *a conservative newspaper.*

The *Military Times*, a liberal Gannett publication favoring inclusion of professed homosexuals in the military, has just released an astonishing poll of active-duty subscribers. Results of the 2008 annual survey indicate that success for that cause essentially would destroy the volunteer force.

Survey Results

As in previous years, the annual *Military Times Poll* reveals that approximately 58% of respondents are opposed to efforts to repeal what the survey described as the "Don't Ask, Don't Tell policy." The catchphrase incorrectly labels the 1993 law, Section 654, Title 10, which clearly states that homosexuals are not eligible to be in the military.

The 2008 *Military Times Poll* asked a new question that produced jaw-dropping results: "If the 'don't ask, don't tell' policy is overturned and gays are allowed to serve openly, how would you respond?" The article emphasized that 71% of respondents said they would continue to serve. But almost 10% said "I would not re-enlist or extend my service," and 14% said "I would consider not re-enlisting or extending my service." Only 6% expressed "No Opinion." Before voting to repeal the law, Section 654, Title 10, members of Congress, and President-elect Barack Obama, ought to do the math.

Troop Losses

If the opinions of Reserve and National Guard troops are similar to those of active-duty personnel surveyed in the *Military Times Poll,* and if the poll's findings approximate the number of military people who would leave or consider leaving if the 1993 law is repealed, combined losses (including Guard and Reserve forces) would be huge.

- A rough estimate using Defense Department numbers for all service branches and components, totaling more than 2 million, indicates that a loss of one in ten (almost 10%) would cost the military approximately 228,600 people—more than the active-duty Marine Corps (200,000).

- If an additional 14% decided to leave, the voluntary exodus would translate into a loss of almost 527,000—a figure approaching the size of today's active-duty Army (more than 545,000).

- Estimates of losses in active-duty forces alone would range between 141,000 (10%) and 323,000 (23%).

The poll's findings are not an exact prediction, but they are significant and ought to be of great concern to President-elect Barack Obama and members of Congress who are considering a vote to repeal the 1993 law. If that legislation succeeds, the Defense Department's new policy would be forced cohabitation with homosexuals, 24/7, in all military communities, to include Army and Marine infantry, Special Operations Forces, Navy SEALS, and submarines.

Corollary programs to make the new policy "work" would include professional "diversity training" to enforce acceptance, and "zero tolerance" of anyone who disagrees. Dissenters would face discipline and be denied promotions, which would end their military careers. Incidents of misconduct would increase threefold, to include male/male and female/female misconduct that undermines discipline and demoralizes the troops. These results would harm recruiting and retention, and effectively destroy the volunteer force.

Other Polls

Advocates of repealing the law always point to professional civilian polls that appear to support their cause, but they have been confounded by the annual *Military Times* surveys, which have always been more credible.

> *There is no "national security" argument for repealing a law designed to protect good order and discipline in military living conditions offering little or no privacy.*

Professional pollsters recognize that survey respondents who think that a policy is already in place are more likely to favor it. Military personnel, however, are more likely than civilians to know what the 1993 law actually says, and why. Hence the disparity between the *Military Times* annual polls and several highly publicized civilian polls asking confused questions about [former President] Bill Clinton's convoluted "Don't Ask, Don't Tell" policy. Civilian polls, like the one done last July [2008] by the *Washington Post* usually limit their inquiries to personal feelings about homosexuals (which are usually positive), or ask whether gays should serve openly or discreetly.

The December 2006 news release announcing the often-quoted Zogby Poll on this subject, which was paid for by the Center for the Study of Sexual Minorities in the Military (now called the Michael D. Palm Center), blatantly spun the story by omitting mention of responses to the key question asked—Should homosexuals serve openly in the military? The 26% of

Zogby respondents who favored repeal of the law could not compete with the combined 69% of people who said that they were opposed or neutral on that question. This was hardly a mandate for radical cultural change in the military.

There is no record of any poll seeking to gauge opinions on the actual consequences of repealing the law; forced co-habitation with homosexuals in all military communities, 24/7, with "zero tolerance" of dissent.

The *Military Times Poll* also indicates that 60% of the active-duty troops surveyed are "Wary of Obama." The newspaper's webpage posted a video of Obama talking about his intent to convince the troops that he knows what he is doing. It does not help to know, however, that high-level members of Obama's Transition Team are meeting with leaders of the LGBT (Lesbian, Gay, Bisexual, Transgender) Left to discuss administration appointments and legislative goals.

No Reason for Repeal

There is no "national security" argument for repealing a law designed to protect good order and discipline in military living conditions offering little or no privacy. Federal courts have upheld the constitutionality of the statute several times, and it continues to enjoy strong support among military men and women. Regardless of what it is called, the 1993 law, Section 654, Title 10, deserves continued support.

Contrary to some disingenuous news reports, activists for gays in the military are determined to impose their agenda on our military. They are working with the incoming administration and pushing hard for repeal. Members of Congress and the new Commander-in-Chief need to take this issue seriously, and see to it that activists demanding repeal of the law do not win.

US Marines Overwhelmingly Oppose the Repeal of "Don't Ask Don't Tell"

Mark Walker

Mark Walker is a reporter for the North County Times, *a local newspaper serving the northern parts of San Diego County in California.*

Nearly 7 of every 10 Marines in combat roles say repealing the policy that prohibits gays and lesbians from serving openly would harm their unit's effectiveness, more than any other branch of the armed forces, according to a long-awaited Pentagon survey released Tuesday [November 30, 2010].

Forty-four percent of all service members said unit effectiveness would be harmed by its repeal; among the Marines whose jobs are on the front lines, that number rose to 67 percent.

"Among the services, the Marines were consistently more negative in their responses about the effect of repeal," the report said.

The survey ordered by Defense Secretary Robert Gates concludes that the armed services as a whole would see little disruption by repealing the 17-year-old policy of "don't ask, don't tell."

The policy prohibits the military from asking service members about their sexual orientation and forbids troops from engaging in homosexual activity or revealing whether they are gay or lesbian.

For the more than 14,000 troops who have been discharged under the policy, the report recommends they have a path for rejoining the military.

Marine Corps Resistance

A repeal could have dramatic, long-term consequences in this region [San Diego County], home to more than 75,000 Marines and sailors at Camp Pendleton and Miramar Marine Corps Air Station. The region also is home to tens of thousands of sailors stationed in the San Diego area, and thousands of military retirees.

The Marine Corps' resistance [to repeal of DADT] has come from the top down.

A repeal of the ban would affect base housing and military benefits.

Gates, who supports ending the law that was adopted during the [Bill] Clinton administration, said it won't happen overnight, even if the U.S. Senate goes along with President Barack Obama's call for its end. The House of Representatives has already approved repealing it.

"It would be unwise to push ahead with full implementation of repeal before more can be done to prepare the force, in particular those ground combat specialties and units, for what could be a disruptive and disorienting change," Gates said.

The Marine Corps' resistance has come from the top down. Former Commandant Gen. James Conway was a staunch opponent, and his successor, Gen. James Amos, says he believes it could be disruptive to troops at war in Afghanistan.

Amos also has cited the Marine Corps' policy of assigning two troops to a room on its bases as a potential problem.

But Gates said housing and spousal benefit policies for service members "can and should be applied equally to homosexuals as well as heterosexuals."

Gates also said he does not expect the Pentagon would have to rethink those policies to accommodate gays if they are allowed to serve openly. A majority of concerns could be addressed through increased training and education, he said.

About one-quarter of the more than 16,000 Marines who responded to the survey said they serve with someone whom they know to be homosexual.

North County resident and former Camp Pendleton Marine Evelyn Thomas has long fought for the policy's repeal. She said that it will take more than just political will.

"The military is going to have to have some time to prepare and provide some form of protection for people to serve openly," said Thomas, a lesbian who left the Marine Corps in 2004.

About one-quarter of the more than 16,000 Marines who responded to the survey said they serve with someone whom they know to be homosexual.

Max Disposti, president of the North County Lesbian, Gay, Bisexual and Transgender Coalition, said his group believes the survey was flawed.

"The questions were meant to create a problem to begin with by asking troops and their families how they would feel if their husband or wife worked next to a gay or lesbian," he said. "We have opposed, since the beginning, framing questions in a way that asks if discrimination should continue."

How lawmakers analyze the survey is what Disposti wants to see.

Republican Responses

"Will they look for another excuse to postpone repeal, or will they agree with the majority of the population?" he said, adding he considers the ban on gays similar to the military's policy that once segregated black and white troops.

North County congressional Reps. Darrell Issa, R-Vista, and Brian Bilbray, R-Solana Beach, say they do not believe it is time to change the policy.

"Making any changes to current policy during wartime must be done with extreme caution," Bilbray said.

That same position is held by Rep. Duncan Hunter, R-El Cajon, a Marine reservist who served two combat tours in Iraq and one in Afghanistan before being elected to Congress in 2008. Issa, Bilbray and Hunter all opposed the House bill that included the repeal.

Hunter received a briefing from Pentagon officials Tuesday morning. He said they told him that the Marine Corps "has to be approached with extreme caution on this issue" because of its troops' general resistance to the repeal.

The second-term congressman acknowledged the policy will probably be repealed someday, but not with his support.

"I believe it affects unit cohesiveness, and front-line men and women simply should not have to worry about this," he said. "The military is the wrong place for a social experiment, and repeal doesn't make the military any better, but it will affect good order and discipline."

Slightly more than 115,000 troops overall responded to the survey, along with more than 44,000 military spouses.

Senate Democrats plan to force a vote in December. Senate Republicans were generally silent after release of the report.

Report highlights include:

- Troops kicked out of service under "don't ask, don't tell" should be allowed to reapply under the same criteria as others seeking re-entry into the armed forces.

  - The report does not recommend that sexual orientation be placed alongside race, color, religion, sex and national origin as a class eligible for various diversity programs and for resolving complaints.

- No special arrangement would be made for those with religious or moral objections to serving alongside gays. People of differing moral values and religious convictions already serve together, it says.

The Chiefs of the Armed Forces Oppose Repealing "Don't Ask Don't Tell"

John McCormack

John McCormack is a staff writer for The Weekly Standard, *a conservative political magazine.*

The heads of the Army, Marines, Air Force, and Navy oppose the current amendment to repeal "don't ask, don't tell" [DADT]. Senator John McCain's office just released letters from the chiefs of the armed services, as well as a statement from the senator urging Congress to let the military complete its study before taking legislative action.

"I cannot overemphasize the importance of completing the comprehensive review prior to taking any legislative action," says McCain. "Our military is currently engaged in two wars and we need to have a true assessment of the impact of repealing 'Don't Ask Don't Tell' on battlefield effectiveness prior to taking any legislative action. We must remain focused on what is in the best interest of our service men and women and not simply fulfill a campaign promise."

McCain has written a letter to [Senator Carl] Levin [chairman of the Senate Armed Services Committee] opposing repeal. Here are excerpts from the service chiefs' letters:

"I remain convinced that it is critically important to get a better understanding of where our Soldiers and Families are on this issue, and what the impacts on readiness and unit cohesion might be, so that I can provide informed military advice to the President and the Congress," said General George W. Casey, Jr., U.S. Army. "I also believe that repealing the law before the completion of the review will be seen by the men and women of the Army as a reversal of our commitment to hear their views before moving forward."

"We need this review to fully assess our force and carefully examine potential impacts of a change in the law. My concern is that legislative changes at this point, regardless of the precise language used, may cause confusion on the status of the law in the Fleet and disrupt the review process itself by leading Sailors to question whether their input matters," said Admiral [Gary] Roughead, U.S. Navy.

It is critically important to get a better understanding of where our Soldiers and Families are on this issue, and what the impacts on readiness and unit cohesion might be.

"I encourage the Congress to let the process the Secretary of Defense created to run its course. Collectively, we must make logical and pragmatic decisions about the long-term policies of our Armed Forces—which so effectively defend this great nation," said General James T. Conway, Commandant of the U.S. Marine Corps.

"I believe it is important, a matter of keeping faith with those currently serving in the Armed Forces, that the Secretary of Defense-commissioned review be completed before there is any legislation to repeal the DA/DT law. Such action allows me to provide the best military advice to the President, and sends an important signal to our Airmen and their families that their opinion matters. To do otherwise, in my view, would be presumptive and would reflect an intent to act before all relevant factors are assessed, digested and understood," said General Norton A. Schwartz, U.S. Air Force.

Current
CONTROVERSIES

CHAPTER 4

What Will Be the Impact of Gays Serving Openly in the US Military?

Chapter Preface

Congress's 2010 repeal of "Don't Ask Don't Tell"—the policy that allowed gays to serve in the military as long as they did not reveal their homosexual status—was hailed by gay rights advocates as a great victory in the struggle to achieve equality for gay men, lesbians, bisexuals, and transsexuals; however, the gay community has a number of other important goals, one of which is for marriage between two persons of the same sex to eventually be legally recognized in the United States. A few states have allowed gay marriages, but a majority of states as well as the US Congress have passed laws defining marriage as a legal union between heterosexuals. The battle for gay marriage, therefore, appears to be a formidable one.

Gay advocates say that denying gays the right to be legally married is discrimination based on sexual orientation because it denies gays all of the legal, financial, and emotional benefits of marriage available to heterosexual couples. Failing to allow gay marriages, they argue, also stigmatizes the children of gay parents. Opposition to gay marriage, many people contend, is rooted in antigay attitudes similar to the racial bigotry that was common in America surrounding interracial marriages during earlier civil rights struggles. Gay marriage opponents, on the other hand, argue that marriage should be limited to heterosexual couples because traditionally, and under many religions, marriages are entered into for the purpose of procreation. Gays, many people insist, could achieve equal or similar rights under the law via legislation that could create civil unions—basically another term for same-sex partnerships—or otherwise provide domestic partner rights.

Many in the gay community, however, reject any solution other than the full right to legal marriage, and the issue of gay marriage is gaining the attention of legislatures and courts around the nation. The US Congress in 1996 enacted the Federal Defense of Marriage Act (DOMA), which defines marriage as a legal union between one man and one woman for purposes of all federal laws and provides that states need not recognize a marriage from another state if it is between persons of the same sex. DOMA has been applied to deny same-sex couples the rights given to heterosexual married couples in terms of Social Security benefits, hospital visitation rights, and other spousal rights. Since then, a number of states have enacted similar legislation. Today, about thirty-nine states have some type of law that protects traditional marriage and prohibits gay marriage, many in the form of state constitutional amendments. Only a handful of states issue marriage licenses to gay couples—Massachusetts, Connecticut, New Hampshire, Iowa, Vermont, New York, and the District of Columbia.

Despite this wall of opposition, gay advocates have recently seen some progress in their fight for gay marriage. In February 2011, President Barack Obama ordered the US Justice Department to stop defending the federal DOMA. The president's decision came in response to lawsuits that have challenged Section 3 of DOMA, which defines marriage as only between a man and a woman. As explained by US attorney general Eric Holder, the president believes that Section 3 is unconstitutional because it violates the equal protection guaranteed under the Due Process clause of the Fifth Amendment to the US Constitution.

Litigation challenging DOMA and similar state laws may ultimately reach the US Supreme Court, according to legal experts. One high-profile case that could reach the nation's highest court is *Perry v. Schwarzenagger*, which challenges California's Proposition 8 ballot initiative to deny marriage to gay couples. Filed by famed lawyers Ted Olson and David Boies, who were opponents in the litigation following the 2000 presidential election, *Perry v. Schwarzenagger* claims that Proposition 8 is an unconstitutional violation of equal protection and due process. On August 4, 2010, Olson and Boies scored their first victory when US District judge Vaughn Walker ruled in their favor. Judge Walker found Proposition 8 unconstitutional because there is no rational basis for denying same-sex couples the right to marry. The court noted that before Proposition 8 was passed, California had already issued eighteen thousand marriage licenses to same-sex couples without any showing of harm. The case has now been appealed to the Ninth Circuit Court of Appeals, and the next step may be the Supreme Court.

The road ahead for gays in America remains uncertain, but if the victory in repealing "Don't Ask Don't Tell" is followed by a Supreme Court decision upholding gay marriage, gay advocates will have succeeded in breaking down significant barriers that have stigmatized and restricted homosexuals for a very long time.

Gays in the Military Must Remain Closeted Until Repeal Takes Effect

David Wood

David Wood is a war correspondent for Politics Daily, *an online newsmagazine (now part of* The Huffington Post)*, with extensive experience reporting on conflict, national security, and foreign affairs issues.*

What happens now that Congress has voted to repeal the 'don't ask, don't tell' [DADT] ban on gays in the military? Nothing.

DADT Still the Law

For the next few months and possibly for as long as a year, gays and lesbians in uniform will still be subject to investigation and discharge if they acknowledge their sexual orientation, Pentagon officials said. Despite action in Congress to repeal it, the controversial policy banning gays from serving openly remains in effect until, in essence, the Defense Department is good and ready to wipe if off the books. The Pentagon issued a directive [on December 18, 2010,] from its personnel chief, Clifford Stanley, alerting troops worldwide to the Senate vote to join the U.S. House in approving legislation to repeal DADT. The directive was expected to emphasize that the law itself has not been immediately repealed, and that the current regulations banning gays and lesbians from serving openly in the military remain in place.

"Once this legislation is signed into the law by the president, the Department of Defense will immediately proceed with the planning necessary to carry out this change carefully and methodically, but purposefully," Defense Secretary Robert Gates said. Change is coming, Gates said, but the current policy stays in place during an implementation process.

The law itself will not be effectively pulled down until the Pentagon has had a chance to adjust regulations that relate to same-sex partners, including next-of-kin notification, family access to commissaries and military fitness centers, health insurance and other benefits.

The Defense Department also plans to conduct training of all military personnel to emphasize current standing orders that every member is to be treated with dignity and respect regardless of gender, religion, color and other differences. When all that is completed—a process that Gates has said could take up to a year—actual repeal won't happen until the president, the Secretary of Defense and chairman of the Joint Chiefs of Staff all certify that it will not negatively affect combat readiness.

> The law itself will not be effectively pulled down until the Pentagon has had a chance to adjust regulations that relate to same-sex partners.

Even then—still not done. According to the repeal legislation, a 60-day waiting period will follow the formal certification. At the end of those two months, gays and lesbians will be able to serve openly in the armed services without discrimination.

Until then, "don't ask, don't tell" will remain in effect—"it's still the law," Pentagon spokesman Col. David Lapan told reporters.

A Careful Implementation Process

Gates has promised that the Pentagon won't "slow-roll" this process—because the number one advocate pushing for repeal of the gay ban is the commander in chief, sitting in the White House. President [Barack] Obama, Gates has said, will be keeping "a keen eye" on the Pentagon's progress as it works to carry out a new policy.

The Defense Department also plans to conduct training of all military personnel to emphasize . . . that every member is to be treated with dignity and respect.

The Pentagon plan to implement the historic change is laid out like a military campaign, with stages and steps and benchmarks—although it is vague about how long it will take.

The implementation phase, the plan says, "would last until some point after the effective date of repeal, once the roll-out of new policies has been completed." During implementation, the Defense Department and the Armed Services would finalize the new policies and then begin "education and training programs necessary to prepare the force for repeal and to communicate the upcoming policy changes." After all of that, "upon the effective date of repeal," the military "would put any new or revised policies into effect."

Of course, all this careful fandango could be thrown into chaos if federal courts conclude that DADT is unconstitutional and order an immediate lifting of the ban. That could come as early as this spring [2011], when a U.S. appellate court is expected to rule on a lower court finding that DADT is unconstitutional and should be immediately lifted. That order has been stayed pending the review by the 9th District Court of Appeals.

Until then, gays and lesbians in the military are being advised to continue to serve under cover. The mechanisms to discharge them are still in place, although no gays or lesbians have actually been discharged under new regulations put in place by Defense Secretary Gates in October [2010], making the discharge process more cumbersome and time consuming.

The Logistics of Integrating Openly Gay Service Members Will Not Be Easy

Rod Powers

Rod Powers, a retired Air Force first sergeant with twenty-two years of active-duty service, is a writer and author who covers US military issues for About.com, an online information website owned by The New York Times Company.

The issue of gays in the military has been a hot political debate ever since the beginning of "Don't Ask, Don't Tell." For the most part, liberals wish to allow gays to openly serve in the armed forces, while conservatives wish to keep the current "Don't Ask, Don't Tell" policy, or wish to ban gays from serving in the military outright.

The Policy

The military didn't make up the "Don't Ask,' Don't Tell" policy. The military has no choice but to obey federal laws enacted by Congress and Executive Orders directed by the Commander-in-Chief (The President).

When President [Bill] Clinton was running for office, the Department of Defense (DOD) had a policy, which prohibited homosexuals from serving in the military. If one was even suspected to be homosexual (whether or not they were actively engaging in homosexual conduct), they were investigated, and (if determined to be homosexual) discharged. Sometimes they were court-martialed. Often, they received Article 15s [nonjudicial punishment, a type of military discipline] along with their discharge.

Clinton promised (as a campaign promise) to eliminate the restrictions about homosexuals serving in the military.

When he was elected to office, he set about trying to make this happen, by drafting an Executive Order which would have ordered the Secretary of Defense to eliminate the policy.

This worried the members of Congress who introduced legislation which would have made the DOD policy into Federal Law, that Clinton (nor any other President) would not be able to over-ride. It was very clear that not only did Congress have enough votes to pass the law, but they had enough votes to over-ride any possible Presidential veto.

Clinton was now between a rock and a hard place. If he tried to enact an Executive Order, Congress would pass their legislation, and he could not afford (politically) to have his first veto over-ridden by Congress.

So, the negotiations began, which ultimately resulted in Clinton issuing an Executive Order for the current "Don't Ask, Don't Tell" policy. In exchange, Congress dropped the legislation which would have made a federal law, forever forbidding homosexuals to serve.

The people who criticize the ["Don't Ask Don't Tell"] policy either have no significant military experience, or, their military experience is limited to the relatively luxurious privileges of the commissioned officer.

Under "Don't Ask, Don't Tell," the military no longer asks a person's sexual preference when that person enlists (it used to be a question on the enlistment forms). The military no longer investigates claims that a person is homosexual (they can, and do, however, investigate allegations of homosexual conduct).

Homosexual conduct is still grounds for discharge (honorable). Conduct includes, not only homosexual acts while on active duty, but also includes telling others that you are homosexual (That's the "Don't Tell" part).

President [Barack] Obama campaigned with a promise to replace the "Don't Ask, Don't Tell" policy with one that allows gays and lesbians to serve openly in the military. However, after taking office, he has failed to keep his promise thus far. In a recent interview, Obama stated that now is not yet the time. You have to assume that the President (as Commander-In-Chief) is briefed often on this matter by the highest ranking military officials (and those guys are pretty sharp cookies). In fact, the current Obama administration is planning on fighting a recent Federal court ruling which declares "Don't Ask, Don't Tell" to be unconstitutional. You have to ask yourself, "Why would the Obama administration fight against a ruling they were initially in favor of?"

What I fail to understand is exactly how the military would be expected to house openly-admitted homosexuals without seriously violating the sexual privacy rights of the heterosexual majority, or causing major problems with morale.

I would suspect that President Obama has been convinced of all the problems it would create if the policy was changed at this time. I have been contacted by several current military members who state that they would get out of the military if gays and lesbians were allowed to serve openly. My User Comment section on this issue is flooded with opinions stating passionate feelings about both sides of the debate.

Difficult Logistics

What bothers me is that most of the people who criticize the policy either have no significant military experience, or, their military experience is limited to the relatively luxurious privileges of the commissioned officer.

Single commissioned officers who reside on-base are authorized to reside in single rooms. That makes all the difference in the world. But, what about the poor, low-rank, enlisted person, who is forced to live in the barracks with a roommate? Isn't anyone concerned at all about the privacy rights of the single, low-ranking heterosexual?

I will be the first to admit that homosexuals have served in the military for generations. I will also stipulate that most have served with honor and distinction. I will further admit that the relatively minor problems which would arise in the workplace could be effectively handled.

> One thing supporters of this change fail to realize is that there is NO RIGHT to serve in the U.S. Military.

What I fail to understand is exactly how the military would be expected to house openly-admitted homosexuals, in an environment where we force people to room together, without seriously violating the sexual privacy rights of the heterosexual majority, or causing major problems with morale.

One thing supporters of this change fail to realize is that there is NO RIGHT to serve in the U.S. Military. The military is allowed, by law, to determine who is suitable for their purposes, and who is not. For example, if you have had or have a medical condition which (in the opinion of the military, not your own) would cause problems, the military will not accept you. If you score low on the military entrance test (ASVAB), the military will not accept you. If you have too many kids, you can't get in. If you didn't graduate from high school, or made some minor criminal mistakes as a younger person, don't bother to apply.

Gay Military Members Would Still Be Dismissed for Sexual Misconduct

Bill Keith

Bill Keith is a writer for Suite101.com, an online information source and writers' network.

Serving openly gay may mean that the service member will be held to conduct standards lifted from the past when the member could not serve openly gay.

Since Congress passed the gay ban repeal rescinding the 17-year old [Bill] Clinton era, "Don't Ask Don't Tell" [DADT] policy, congressional and military leaders have worked for several weeks to determine how and when the new policy will take shape. As described in a recent ABC News online article, January 29, 2011, "Military Lays Out Plan to Implement Gay Ban Repeal", written by Lolita C. Baldor and Pauline Jelinek, as military leaders develop training, further policy refinement continues; it may take more than a year to be in place.

Gay Members Serving Faithfully

The December 1, 2010 article in the *New York Daily News* by Michael Sheridan and Richard Sisk, "DADT survey reveals military is ok with gay troops, Sec. Def. [Secretary of Defense Robert] Gates urges Congress to repeal policy," details many of results of the survey. Among the statistics, "115,052 active troops surveyed, 69% believe they have already worked alongside a gay service member, and 92% of those said it had a positive impact or no impact on their working relationship."

Military leaders must however deal [with] the policies and procedures that will train and inform the troops sorting out

Bill Keith, "After DADT Repeal, Will Gay Military Members Still Be Dismissed?" Suite101.com, January 29, 2011. Copyright © 2011 by Suite101.com. All rights reserved. Reproduced by permission of the author.

wide ranging issues from sleeping arrangements, gay married accommodation, and harassment and discrimination issues.

["Don't Ask Don't Tell"] dismissed gay military members for being gay, but to be truly fair the new policy would dismiss gay members for sexual misconduct.

Military Culture Needs Change

While the survey indicates that today's military member is more accepting of homosexuals working alongside them, the military's overall culture must make some changes to successfully implement the policy change. Currently, the military molds its members to be part of an integrated ... team and subordinating individual needs to meet the needs of the mission. This presumably would not change.

With its emphasis on conformity, serving openly gay would seem to be at odds with decades-old military codes and processes supporting the belief that "homosexuality is incompatible with military service," which is the underlying position for DADT. What will be interesting is how the new policy will distinguish between the homosexual person and homosexual behavior.

Without knowing ... how the changes will be finally codified, the focus of these new policies and guidance must also balance individual rights and military conformity. In nearly all cases, the military focuses on getting the mission accomplished. So, the policy must then navigate a precarious line defining sexual misconduct.

Duty in the Combat Zone

When in garrison, the military stateside work environment resembles that of any large company. However, the military work environment underwent transformation in the 1980s and 1990s after changes in public law increased opportunities for women in the military workplace. Additionally, the 1991 Tailhook Scandal [regarding rampant sexual harassment at a military conference] highlighted the need for serious changes needed in military culture on the role of women in the military.

Nascent sexual harassment awareness training guidance released by military leaders of that era intended to combat problems in the workplace. This training certainly helped many individuals understand that their actions or words could potentially create a hostile work environment for the team.

Serving openly gay in the future could mean that the service member will be held to conduct standards rooted in the past when the member could not serve openly gay.

Although these programs are more effective and comprehensive today, anecdotally there were instances where the easily offended or poorly trained inadvertently created a reverse hostile environment where the male members of the unit became overly cautious to work with females, out [of] fear of an accusation.

Fear of sexual harassment accusations also allowed certain ambitious individuals the ability to gain an advantage over the unit by purposely using a climate of fear. In other accounts, one trainee forced schedulers to completely change training schedules to suit her needs while another sought to get the choice duty assignment over her counterparts. Fortunately, this type of behavior did not represent the norm.

Dismissed for Sexual Misconduct

If the new policies focus on protecting homosexuals as a class, then those policies may wind up hurting the ones being protected because the culture demands conformity rather than special privileges.

If the policies lean toward effective military operations, then all service members will adhere to similar standards that will blend into military culture well. DADT dismissed gay military members for being gay, but to be truly fair the new policy would dismiss gay members for sexual misconduct, provided the leaders adequately define sexual misconduct. It would then seem counterintuitive that serving openly gay in the future could mean that the service member will be held to conduct standards rooted in the past when the member could not serve openly gay.

Gay Service Members' Rights Are Not Yet Equal

Ed O'Keefe

Ed O'Keefe is a staff writer for The Washington Post, *a daily newspaper published in Washington, D.C.*

The military dismissed Marquell Smith in 2006 for violating its "don't ask, don't tell" [DADT] policy, giving him a less-than-honorable discharge that made the former Marine ineligible for a veteran's hiring preference used by federal agencies where he hoped to work.

After more than three years of appeals, the Defense Department reversed course and gave him an honorable discharge. In the interim, "there was a little bit of reluctance by employers to hire me, I think, especially since they couldn't give me veteran's preference," Smith said. "You miss out on opportunities."

Worse, "I was confronted by potential employers asking why I was out of the military," he said. "I had to come out and tell them that I was discharged under 'don't ask, don't tell.' It creates an awkward conversation."

Smith, 30, is back in school and plans to apply for new jobs when he graduates, or maybe reenlist in the military. Troops discharged for violating the gay ban may reenlist once President [Barack] Obama and military leaders officially end the ban—probably later this year [2011], as the president recently promised. (About 13,000 troops have been discharged for violating "don't ask, don't tell.")

Continuing Problems for Gays

But Smith's experience symbolizes the types of issues current and former troops who are gay are likely to confront even after the ban ends. Gay rights leaders said they are preparing for several more years of work to ensure gay troops and those kicked out for violating the ban earn the same rights and protections afforded to straight colleagues.

Groups who led last year's campaign to repeal "don't ask, don't tell" now want Obama to sign an executive order extending nondiscriminatory protections to gay troops. They're also pushing the Pentagon to eventually extend housing and health-care benefits to the same-sex partners of openly gay service members and hope the military will make it easier for discharged troops such as Smith to earn a job, by removing any mention of homosexuality from discharge papers.

So far, the White House and Pentagon aren't budging.

> Gay rights leaders said they are preparing for several more years of work to ensure gay troops . . . earn the same rights and protections afforded to straight colleagues.

White House aides would not say whether Obama plans to issue any orders extending nondiscriminatory protections to gay troops, pointing instead to Pentagon policies set to take effect once the ban is lifted. The new language will state that all troops are "entitled to an environment free from personal, social, or institutional barriers" preventing promotion and that "harassment or abuse based on sexual orientation is unacceptable."

"The release of the policy guidance is an important step toward implementing repeal of 'don't ask, don't tell,'" White House spokesman Shin Inouye said. "As the president said in his State of the Union address, DADT will be fully repealed this year."

The Need for an Executive Order

But activists such as Richard Socarides say the lack of an executive order means gay troops would have fewer legal protections than civilians working for the Pentagon and other federal agencies.

"If you work at the Agriculture Department as a clerk, you have better protections than somebody in the military," said Socarides, a former gay rights adviser to [US president] Bill Clinton and director of Equality Matters. "They ought to be the same."

A presidential executive order brings the weight of the Oval Office, activists say. [US president] Harry Truman used an executive order to begin the full integration of black troops, and gay rights activists want Obama to issue similar orders protecting gay troops from discrimination in the ranks. They note that Clinton and Obama issued executive orders and memos extending nondiscriminatory protections and benefits to gay federal employees and their spouses.

"This last final step is not a small matter," Socarides added. "It's crucial that gay military personnel have legally enforceable protections which are lasting over time."

Obama, who vowed during his campaign to end "don't ask, don't tell," demanded that Congress lift the ban through legislation because lawmakers had enacted it with legislation. He could have ordered the military to stop enforcing the policy, or to use it in more limited circumstances, but White House aides [in 2010] cautioned that future presidents could reverse Obama's orders by using the same presidential powers.

As for pay and benefits, the federal Defense of Marriage Act bars the Pentagon from extending full health-care and housing access to same-sex partners, but civilian federal agencies now provide relocation pay, access to day-care centers and gyms, and permit paid leave for gay workers caring for ill partners, among other benefits.

Pentagon officials plan to identify similar benefits, and should do so quickly, according to Aubrey Sarvis, executive director of the Servicemembers Legal Defense Network (SLDN).

"I think some at the Pentagon are going to be very uncomfortable when they have to face the realities of pay and benefits, because some will be treated differently based on their sexual orientation," he said. "In this post-repeal world, we've moved beyond someone being fired for their sexual orientation, but we're bumping up against the reality that they'll receive different pay and benefits."

Renewing Gay Discharges

Among the difficult challenges is the push to get the Pentagon to erase any mention of homosexual conduct from the records of the 13,000 troops discharged for violating the ban.

"Many will want to see that removed," Sarvis said, noting that hundreds of former service members have called his offices asking whether the Defense Department might remove references to "don't ask, don't tell" now that the ban is ending. SLDN, which provides legal services to troops affected by the ban, is pushing Defense Secretary Robert M. Gates to establish special boards that would review the discharges and at least grant an honorable discharge to those who didn't receive it.

The Pentagon is reviewing the proposal, but it does permit troops to appeal their dismissal to discharge review boards, according to spokeswoman Eileen Lainez.

"This is going to be a continual process over years of kind of changing the mentality," said Fred Sainz, vice president of the Human Rights Campaign, another group that pushed for repeal. "I think that as frustrating as it is for many, we got as good as we were going to get, and people who are realistic about these things understand that. Over the course of the next few years, we'll work on this cycle of continuous improvement."

Partners of Gay Service Members Will Not Receive Military Spouse Benefits

Bryant Jordan

Bryant Jordan is an associate editor for Military.com, a military and veterans membership organization whose website provides information about military issues.

Regardless of the [Barack] Obama administration's decision not to defend the law defining marriage as a heterosexual union, the U.S. military won't be extending spousal benefits to same-sex couples, the Defense Department says.

Pentagon spokesman Col. David Lapan said the federal Defense of Marriage Act [DOMA] remains on the books and the military will continue to follow it after repeal of Don't Ask, Don't Tell [DADT] is fully implemented.

"Basically DOMA remains in effect [for the military] unless Congress repeals it or a court action strikes it down," Lapan said.

DOMA and Repeal of DADT

Signed into law by President Bill Clinton in 1996, the Defense of Marriage Act strictly defines "marriage" as a union between a man and woman. The law has often been cited by opponents of federal spousal rights for homosexual couples.

In testimony during Don't Ask, Don't Tell hearings last year [2010], senior defense officials said dumping the law barring gays from serving openly would not result in gay partners shopping at the PX or moving into base housing. Undersecretary of Defense for Personnel and Readiness Clifford Stanley said the military is bound by the DOMA statute. The federal law would also take precedent over same-sex couples who were married in states where homosexual unions are legal, he said.

But Elaine Donnelly, president of the Center for Military Readiness, believes the administration's decision to stop defending the constitutionality of DOMA is but a first step toward sending that law the way of Don't Ask, Don't Tell. She said the Justice Department cited Don't Ask, Don't Tell's repeal in its Feb. 23 [2011] announcement that the marriage law was unconstitutional.

"This is exactly what we predicted—imposition of [homosexual] law and corollary policies in the military would quickly undermine civilian statutes to the contrary," she said. "The votes of people in more than 30 states, defining legal marriage as a bond between a man and a woman, are being overruled by executive fiat."

But some advocates for gays in the military believe there is nothing in the Obama administration's move on DOMA that will change current service benefits.

"DOMA is DOMA. There's nothing the Pentagon can do about that," said R. Clarke Cooper, executive director of the Log Cabin Republicans, a gay rights advocacy group that sued in federal court to have Don't Ask, Don't Tell overturned last year.

Extending spousal benefits to same-sex couples in the military ... "is an inequality that should be addressed."

"I can see how people want to mix the two up, but they are very distinct issues," said Cooper, an Army combat veteran and a former U.N. diplomat under George W. Bush. "Repeal [of DADT] removes the specter or threat of discharge based on sexual orientation. It doesn't mean someone who has a same-sex partner can get benefits."

The DADT repeal will allow gay service members to list partners on their life insurance and to be notified in the event of emergencies, he said, things that previously would have raised eyebrows and drawn career-ending attention to a gay servicemember, he said.

Spousal Benefits May Take a While

Cooper believes the decision by Obama is purely political, something "to energize the base." Most people have no interest in getting rid of the Defense of Marriage Act, he said.

"The number one issue for voters is the economy, reduction of government spending, reining in the budget and addressing entitlements," he said.

Aubrey Sarvis, executive director of the Servicemembers Legal Defense Network, one of the groups in the lead of fighting to overturn Don't Ask, Don't Tell, said the Justice Department's announcement does little more than narrow its actions regarding DOMA. The department is not pulling out of cases it already joined, he said; it's just not going to defend it moving forward.

But extending spousal benefits to same-sex couples in the military, he said, "is an inequality that should be addressed."

"We're going to begin to have conversations about this in this Congress," said Sarvis, an Army veteran and former chief counsel for the Senate Commerce Committee. "But I think it'll be awhile for this disparity to get the attention it needs."

The Repeal of "Don't Ask Don't Tell" May Aid Other Gay Rights Efforts

Ben Adler

Ben Adler is a journalist who writes for Newsweek, *a US-based weekly newsmagazine, as well as for other publications.*

When President [Barack] Obama signed the repeal of "don't ask, don't tell" (DADT) Wednesday morning [December 22, 2010], gay rights were expanded in a limited way. Even though gays can now serve openly in the military, advocates for their rights say there's more work to be done. The benefits that accrue to military spouses will not be extended to gay partners, even those who are legally married in their home states. And on the big three goals of the gay-rights movement—marriage, equality, and laws protecting them against employment or public-accommodation discrimination—gays are exactly where they were before. Some states and private companies have adopted progressive policies on gay employees. But in a state with no such protections, a hotel owner can still refuse to let a gay couple book a room, and a business owner is allowed not to hire someone on the basis of his sexual orientation.

A Changing Tide

Even though the [gay] community faces a Republican majority in the House of Representatives, it's optimistic about its chances of getting closer to legally recognized equality across the board. Advocates believe that the DADT repeal will have a trickle-down effect, pushing other policy debates in the right direction.

First off, the DADT repeal brings a sense of cultural affirmation. In the 1990s, with the passage of DADT, as well as the Defense of Marriage Act (DOMA)—which defined marriage at the federal level as being between a man and a woman—the momentum was going in the other direction. But it changed last year when Congress added gays to its list of groups protected against hate crimes. The DADT repeal built on that momentum. "This is the first time Congress has passed a major, historic piece of legislation in the gay-rights area," says Richard Socarides, the president of Equality Matters, a new organization focusing on media messaging in favor of gay rights. "Symbolically, the first is always the most important hurdle to get over, so we're hoping for momentum from this." Socarides says that when politicians who feared a backlash for voting to repeal DADT end up not paying a political price, they will feel more comfortable voting for gay-rights legislation in the future. "People will get used to voting in a certain way," he predicts. "It's a barrier that has been passed."

Advocates believe that the DADT repeal will have a trickle-down effect, pushing other policy debates in the right direction.

Gay-rights advocates are confident that gays serving openly in the military will have a positive effect on how they're perceived by society. "To a gay kid struggling with their orientation, for the first time the federal government sent a message that gays and lesbians should be out and open," says Fred Sainz, a vice president of Human Rights Campaign (HRC), a gay-rights organization. "It's an incredibly powerful statement in its affirmation that will have a tremendous impact on transforming hearts and minds."

The DADT repeal may also change the way specific issues get framed. Consider employment discrimination. The Employment Non-Discrimination Act (ENDA), which would prohibit employers from discriminating against gay or transgendered employees (transgendered individuals are not covered by DADT repeal), failed to pass in this Congress, and Republicans are certain not to move it in the next one. Look ahead a few years, though, to when gay soldiers come home from war, injured or traumatized from serving their country in battle. How will it look if those individuals are unable to get a job because of their sexual orientation? The commercials arguing that ENDA should be passed on their behalf will write themselves, and could be very effective at moving moderate voters. "Once we've said as a government that you shouldn't discriminate in military service, it becomes harder to argue that you should discriminate against gays in other ways," says Socarides.

That same logic may strengthen the argument for gay-marriage rights. The spouse of a gay soldier killed in combat who is denied survivor benefits will demonstrate the cost to gays of serving. Congress could amend the law just passed to provide survivor benefits for gay spouses, and it's plausible that it will do so, even with a Republican majority. Repealing the Defense of Marriage Act altogether would be a much more formidable political challenge, though.

> *The work on DADT repeal is not finished.*

More Battles to Come

Various gay-rights groups have different ideas as to how to capitalize on the current momentum. Equality Matters views the Republican Congress as so hostile to employment-nondiscrimination legislation that the group intends to focus primarily on marriage and to do so at the state level and through the courts. While acknowledging the challenges to passing an employment law, Human Rights Campaign says such a measure is still a top priority. The group also is thinking about how it can make progress on other issues while

John Boehner holds the House speaker's gavel. The three pieces of legislation HRC says Republicans may support: a bill to protect gay students from bullying, extending marriage benefits to partners of gay federal employees, and removal of the tax disadvantages of being a same-sex couple.

And the work on DADT repeal is not finished, either. Since the law does not ban discrimination against gays within the military, it will be up to the Obama administration to impose rules to that effect. "It's lucky for gays and lesbians that the Obama administration has two years to put in such protections, because there's no guarantee the next administration will be supportive," says Jonathan Turley, an expert on constitutional and national-security law at George Washington University. Once in place, nondiscrimination rules are unlikely to be undone by the next administration. Socarides, who served as President Bill Clinton's top adviser on gay issues, says that President [George W.] Bush did not undo the executive orders Clinton used to expand protections around sexual orientation. "Historically, rights get expanded and almost never contracted," says Socarides.

Opponents of gay rights know that, too, which gives them more reason to fight tooth and nail along the way. "There are pitched battles to come," says Sainz. Luckily for the gay-rights agenda, there are plenty of willing soldiers.

Organizations to Contact

The editors have compiled the following list of organizations concerned with the issues debated in this book. The descriptions are derived from materials provided by the organizations. All have publications or information available for interested readers. The list was compiled on the date of publication of the present volume; the information provided here may change. Be aware that many organizations take several weeks or longer to respond to inquiries, so allow as much time as possible.

American Civil Liberties Union (ACLU)
125 Broad St., 18th Floor, New York, NY   10004
(212) 549-2500
website: www.aclu.org

The American Civil Liberties Union is an organization that fights in courts, legislatures, and communities to defend and preserve the individual rights and liberties guaranteed by the US Constitution and laws of the United States. The ACLU also works to extend rights to segments of the population that have traditionally been denied their rights, including people of color; women; lesbians, gay men, bisexuals and transgender people; prisoners; and people with disabilities. The group's Lesbian, Gay, Bisexual & Transgender Project (LGBT Project) fights discrimination and influences public opinion through litigation, legislation, and public education across five issue areas: relationships, youth and schools, parenting, gender identity and expression, and discrimination in employment, housing, and other areas. A search of the ACLU website produces a number of publications relating to gays in the military and the "Don't Ask Don't Tell" (DADT) policy, including "Repealing DADT and Military Abortion Ban" and "Gays in the Military: Blah, Blah, Blah."

American Veterans for Equal Rights (AVER)
(718) 849-5665
website: http://aver.us/aver/

AVER is a nonprofit, chapter-based association of active, re-serve, and veteran service members dedicated to full and equal rights and equitable treatment for all present and former members of the US Armed Forces. The group seeks to educate policymakers and the public about gays in the military, and its website is a source of publications on this subject, including press releases, blogs, media articles, and a newsletter, *The For-ward Observer*. Recent press releases, for example, include "Re-peal of Don't Ask Don't Tell" and "Gay Vets Applaud Ban Rul-ing."

Americans For Truth About Homosexuality (AFTAH)
PO Box 5522, Naperville, IL   60567-5522
(630) 546-4439
website: http://americansfortruth.com

Americans For Truth About Homosexuality is a group dedi-cated to exposing and countering the homosexual activist agenda. According to its website, AFTAH seeks to apply the same single-minded determination to opposing the radical homosexual agenda and standing for God-ordained sexuality and the natural family. The AFTAH website has links to nu-merous other antigay and religious websites and to a variety of news articles, a few of them relevant to gays in the military.

Center for Military Readiness (CMR)
PO Box 51600, Livonia, MI   48151
(202) 347-5333
e-mail: info@cmrlink.org
website: www.cmrlink.org

The Center for Military Readiness is an independent, nonpar-tisan, educational organization formed to promote sound military personnel policies in the armed forces. CMR is an al-liance of civilian and active duty and retired military people in all fifty states. One of the issues on the CMR website is gays in the military—a source for numerous articles, most of which oppose the idea of gays serving openly. Examples of recent articles include "Will Senate Surrender Pentagon Social Policies to the 'LGBT Left?'" and "Senate Testimony: European Militaries Are Not Role Models for U.S."

Don't Ask Don't Tell Don't Pursue

Robert Crown Law Library, Stanford Law School
Crown Quadrangle, 559 Nathan Abbott Way
Stanford, CA 94305-8610
website: http://dont.stanford.edu

Don't Ask, Don't Tell, Don't Pursue is a digital law project of the Robert Crown Law Library at Stanford Law School. The Don't Database contains primary materials on the US military's policy on sexual orientation, from World War I to the present, as identified by Professor Janet E. Halley's book, *Don't: A Reader's Guide to the Military's Anti-Gay Policy* (Duke University Press, 1999), including legislation; regulations; internal directives of service branches; materials on particular service members' proceedings (from hearing board transcripts to litigation papers and court decisions); policy documents generated by the military, Congress, the Department of Defense and other offices of the Executive branch; and advocacy documents submitted to government entities.

Family Research Council (FRC)

801 G St. NW, Washington, DC 20001
(800) 225-4008
website: www.frc.org

The Family Research Council is an organization that promotes the conservative values of faith, family, and freedom in public policy and public opinion. FRC's team of experts promotes these core values through policy research, public education on Capitol Hill and in the media, and grassroots mobilization. FRC opposed repeal of the "Don't Ask Don't Tell" (DADT) policy, and a search of the group's website produces articles on gays in the military such as "Opposing View on Gays in the Military: Keep the Law in Place" and "DADT Defeat Doesn't Mean Conservative Surrender."

Heritage Foundation

214 Massachusetts Ave. NE, Washington, DC   20002-4999

(202) 546-4400

website: www.heritage.org

The Heritage Foundation is a conservative research and educational institution—a think tank—whose mission is to formulate and promote conservative public policies based on the principles of free enterprise, limited government, individual freedom, traditional American values, and a strong national defense. The Heritage website publishes reports, factsheets, testimony, commentaries, articles, and blogs about a variety of domestic and foreign policy matters. A search of the website produces several articles on gays in the military, including: "Don't Ask, Don't Tell: Time for Cautious Judgment" and "Don't Ask, I'll Just Tell You What the Law Should Be."

Human Rights Campaign (HRC)

1640 Rhode Island Ave. NW, Washington, DC   20036-3278

(202) 628-4160 • fax: (202) 347-5323

website: www.hrc.org

The Human Rights Campaign is a civil rights organization dedicated to achieving lesbian, gay, bisexual, and transgender (LGBT) equality. By inspiring and engaging all Americans, HRC strives to end discrimination against LGBT citizens and thus realize a nation that achieves fundamental fairness and equality for all. At the federal and state levels, HRC lobbies elected officials, mobilizes grassroots supporters, educates Americans, invests strategically to elect fair-minded officials, and partners with other LGBT organizations. A search of the website produces numerous news articles on the repeal of "Don't Ask Don't Tell.".

Palm Center

Williams Institute, UCLA School of Law, Box 951476

Los Angeles, CA   90095-1476

(310) 825-1432

website: www.palmcenter.org

The Palm Center is a research institute at the University of California committed to sponsoring state-of-the-art scholarship to enhance the quality of public dialogue about critical and controversial issues of the day. For the past decade, the Palm Center's research on sexual minorities in the military has been published in leading social science journals. The Palm Center seeks to be a resource for university-affiliated and independent scholars, students, journalists, opinion leaders, and members of the public. Its website contains a wealth of information and research about various aspects of gays in the military; recent publications, for example, include: *Don't Ask, Don't Tell: Detailing the Cost* and *Presence of Openly Gay Soldiers in IDF Does Not Undermine Unit Social Cohesion.*

US Department of Defense (DoD)

1400 Defense Pentagon, Washington, DC   20301-1400

(703) 571-3343

website: www.defense.gov

The US Department of Defense is America's oldest and largest government agency. Its mission is to provide the military forces needed to deter war and to protect the security of the United States. The department's headquarters is at the Pentagon, a large office building located near Washington, D.C. The goal of the DoD website is to support the overall mission of the Department of Defense by providing official, timely, and accurate information about defense policies, organizations, functions, and operations. Also, the website is the single starting point for finding military information online. The DoD has been closely involved with the issue of repealing the "Don't Ask Don't Tell" policy, and its website is a source of articles and news about the implementation of the repeal legislation. Recent articles include "'Don't Ask' Repeal Training Set to Begin" and "Repeal Plan Progressing Quickly."

Bibliography

Books

William Bonzo

Don't Ask, Do Tell. Charleston, SC: CreateSpace, 2010.

Brandon A. Davis

Don't Ask, Don't Tell: Background and Issues on Gays in the Military. Hauppauge, NY: Nova Science, 2010.

Justin Crockett Elzie

Playing By the Rules. Hulls Cove, ME: Queer Mojo, 2010.

Steve Estes

Ask and Tell: Gay and Lesbian Veterans Speak Out. Chapel Hill, NC: University of North Carolina Press, 2008.

Nathaniel Frank

Unfriendly Fire: How the Gay Ban Undermines the Military and Weakens America. New York: Thomas Dunne Books, 2009.

Richard Ishings

Thesis Supported: Analysis of the Policy Prohibiting Homosexuals from Serving in the US Military. Charleston, SC: CreateSpace, 2009.

Drew D. Jeter

Moral Leadership in an Increasingly Amoral Society: Is the United States Military Value System Suitable in Contemporary America? Washington, DC: LittleWhiteEbook.com, 2010.

Bronson Lemer   *The Last Deployment: How a Gay, Hammer-Swinging Twentysomething Survived a Year in Iraq.* Madison, WI: University of Wisconsin Press, 2011.

James Lord   *My Queer War.* New York: Farrar, Straus & Giroux, 2010.

Anthony Loverde   *A Silent Force: Men and Women Serving Under Don't Ask, Don't Tell.* Bloomington, IN: AuthorHouse, 2010.

Vincent A. Marangoni   *The Impacts of Repealing Don't Ask, Don't Tell.* Hauppauge NY: Nova Science, 2011.

Edward R. Miller-Jones   *Don't Ask, Don't Tell: The Cross-Road Issue of Homosexual Rights.* Beau Bassin, Mauritius: FastBook, 2010.

Jeff Sheng and W.M. Hunt   *Don't Ask, Don't Tell: Volume 1.* Los Angeles, CA: Jeff Sheng Studios, 2010.

G. Dean Sinclair   *Homosexuality and the U.S. Military: A Study of Homosexual Identity and Choice of Military Service.* Saarbrücken, Germany: Lambert, 2010.

Frederic P. Vandome, Agnes F. McBrewster, and John Miller   *Don't Ask, Don't Tell.* Beau Bassin, Mauritius: Alphascript, 2010.

Periodicals and Internet Sources

Adam Amir	"Would Openly Gay Servicemembers Hurt Straight Military Families?" Change.org, August 22, 2010. www.change.org.
Nigel Barber	"Gays Undermine Military Discipline? Best Armies Practice Homosexuality," *Psychology Today*, June 29, 2010. www.psychologytoday.com.
William Buchanan	"Gays in the Military," *Human Events*, May 31, 2010. www.humanevents.com.
Tony Capaccio and Peter S. Green	"Risk 'Low' from Ending Gay Ban in Military, Defense Department Study Says," Bloomberg, November 30, 2010. www.bloomberg.com/news.
Katie Connolly	"How Will the US Military Treat Gay Married Members?" BBC News, January 28, 2011. www.bbc.co.uk/news.
Department of Defense	*Report of the Comprehensive Review of the Issues Associated with a Repeal of "Don't Ask, Don't Tell,"* November 30, 2010. www.defense.gov.
Itamar Eichner	"Follow Israel's Example on Gays in the Military, US Study Says," Ynetnews.com, February 8, 2007. www.ynetnews.com.

David A. Fahrenthold
"For Gay Rights, Is Repeal of 'Don't Ask' Military Ban the End or the Beginning?" *Washington Post*, December 20, 2010. www.washingtonpost.com.

Jody Feder
"'Don't Ask, Don't Tell': A Legal Analysis," Congressional Research Service Reports and Issue Briefs, September 30, 2010. www.fas.org.

FoxNews.com
"Congress Overturns Military Ban of Gays Serving Openly, Sends Bill to Obama's Desk," December 18, 2010.

Gary Gates
"Lesbian, Gay, and Bisexual Men and Women in the US Military: Updated Estimates," The Williams Institute, May 2010. http://williamsinstitute.law.ucla.edu.

Kevin Hechtkopf
"Support for Gays in the Military Depends on the Question," CBS News, February 11, 2010. www.cbsnews.com.

Susan Donaldson James
"Don't Ask, Don't Tell: Gay Soldiers Say Military Changes Are Easy: Pentagon to Review Sexuality Survey, Housing, Benefits, Harassment Policies and More," ABC News, October 22, 2010. http://abcnews.go.com/Health.

Ewen MacAskill "US Military Backs Repeal of Gay 'Don't Ask, Don't Tell' Policy: Ending Gay Policy Would Not Harm Morale, Pentagon Survey Shows," *Guardian* (Manchester, UK), November 30, 2010. www.guardiannews.com.

Merrill A. McPeak "Don't Ask, Don't Tell, Don't Change," *New York Times*, March 4, 2010. www.nytimes.com.

Oliver North "Gays in the Military: Obama's Social Experiment Would Have Devastating Effects on the Finest Military Force the World Has Ever Known," *National Review*, December 7, 2010. www.nationalreview.com.

Ed O'Keefe "Fight for Gays in the Military Isn't Ending Anytime Soon," *Washington Post*, February 10, 2011. http://www.washingtonpost.com/ blogs/federal-eye.

Mackubin Thomas Owens "The Case Against Gays in the Military: Open Homosexuality Would Threaten Unit Cohesion and Military Effectiveness," *Wall Street Journal*, February 2, 2010. http://online.wsj.com.

Rod Powers "Don't Ask, Don't Tell—The Military Policy on Gays," About.com, May 5, 2010. http://usmilitary.about.com.

Radio Free Europe/Radio Liberty "U.S. Military Allows Openly Gay Recruits," March 22, 2011. www.rferl.org.

Rowan Scarborough	"Breaking Ranks on Gays in Military," *Washington Times*, March 1, 2010. www.washingtontimes.com.
Rowan Scarborough	"Combat Troops to Get Gay Sensitivity Training: New Policy OK'd for Battlefield," *Washington Times*, February 24, 2011. www.washingtontimes.com.
John Schwartz	"U.S. Military Moves to Accept Gay Recruits," *New York Times*, October 19, 2010. www.nytimes.com.
Leo Shane III	"GAO: Gay Ban Cost Military $53,000 per Dismissal," *Stars and Stripes*, January 20, 2011. www.stripes.com.
Mark Thompson	"Gays in the Military: Does a Sailor's Murder Signal Deeper Problems?" *Time*, July 7, 2009. www.time.com.
Kayla Webley	"Brief History of Gays in the Military," *Time*, February 2, 2010. www.time.com.
David Wood	"Arguing About Gays in the Military: It's So Over," *Politics Daily*, February 3, 2010. www.politicsdaily.com.

Index

in the military, 35, 59, 76, 94
military policy against, 16, 95
San Diego Police Department, 74
Sarvis, Aubrey, 106, 144
Schwartz, Norton A., 121
Senate (US), 19, 116
Senate Armed Services Committee, 19, 43, 100, 103, 120
Senate Commerce Committee, 144
Service members/troops
DADT impact, 101–102
against gay agenda, 111–114
loss of, 63–64, 83, 112–113
privacy of, 40–42
support for, 82–84
survey of, 111–112
Servicemembers Legal Defense Network (SLDN), 106, 141, 144
Servicemembers United, 106
Sexual assault/harassment, 69, 88, 136
Sexual misconduct, 60, 113, 134–137
Sexual orientation
admitting, 73, 85–86
asking about, 47
concealment of, 78, 84–85
discrimination, 123, 145–147
diversity programs and, 118–119
job effectiveness, 30–32
of lesbian, gay and bisexuals, 28–32
in military, 52
Shalikashvili, John, 77, 93
Sheridan, Michael, 101–102, 134
Sisk, Richard, 101–102, 134
Slovakia, 54
Slovenia, 54–55
Smith, Marquell, 138–139
Snyder, Albert, 22, 24

Snyder v. Phelps, 22–24
Socarides, Richard, 140
Social Security benefits, 124
Sodomy, 16–17, 104
South Africa, 54–55
South Korea, 43
Spain, 54
Spouse benefits, 142–144
Stanley, Clifford, 126
Staver, Matthew, 47
Steinman, Alan M., 94–96
Stenhouse, Todd, 108–110
Support Plan for Implementation, 64
Supreme Court, 23–24
Sweden, 54, 73
Switzerland, 54

T

Tailhook Scandal, 136
Thomas, Evelyn, 117
"Three-tiered" education program, 64
Troops. *See* Service members/troops
Truman, Harry, 140
Turley, Jonathan, 148

U

Ukraine, 54
Uniform Code of Military Justice (UCMJ), 65, 102
Unit cohesion, 78–79, 81
United Arab Emirates, 55
United Kingdom (UK), 54, 60, 90
United Press International, 27–29
United States (US)
honorable service, 94–96